M000251170

KINGDOM LIVING

HOW TO ACTIVATE
YOUR SPIRITUAL AUTHORITY

By Jonas Clark

Unless otherwise noted, Scripture quotations are taken from the King James Version.

Kingdom Living, How to Activate Your Spiritual Authority

ISBN 978-1-886885-21-9

Copyright © 2007 by Jonas Clark

Published by Spirit of Life Publishing
A Great Commission Company
27 West Hallandale Beach Blvd.
Hallandale Beach, Florida
33009-5437, U.S.A.
(954) 456-4420

www.JonasClark.com

Printed in the United States of America
01 02 03 04 05 ¨ 05 04 03 02 01

ABOUT THE AUTHOR

Jonas Clark is a refreshing voice and a champion in the contemporary Church. Jonas served God for more than two decades as a pastor, teacher and evangelist before the Lord called him to his role as an apostle in the end time Church.

An evangelist at heart, Jonas travels around the world preaching the Gospel with a bold apostolic anointing. Fortitude and God's grace have taken his ministry into more than 25 countries, where he delivers a message of salvation, healing, deliverance and apostolic reformation. His passion is to win lost souls for Jesus Christ and equip every believer to take the Good News into the harvest fields to fulfill the Great Commission.

Jonas is the founder of The Global Cause Network, an international network of believers and Champion partners united to build a platform for the apostolic voice. He also heads Spirit of Life Ministries, a multicultural, non-denominational church in Hallandale Beach, Florida.

Jonas is the publisher of *The Voice* magazine, a print media platform that offers Prophetic Revelation for the Apostolic Revolution.

This Book is
Dedicated to...

The builders of Christ's glorious Church.

CONTENTS

Chapter 1
Many believers have a hard time thinking of themselves as kings. For some, suggesting that believers adopt a kingship mentality meets with resistance because it launches negative concepts of unwarranted superiority, abuse of authority, unearned respect, and even an uppity attitude. None of these images, however, convey the intended biblical concept of kingship.

Chapter 2
After Jesus was resurrected, He spent the last 40 days of His earthy ministry talking to His disciples about the Kingdom of God. The emphasis that Jesus placed on imparting the fullness of the Kingdom revelation gives us insight into how important Jesus deemed it to the restoration of all things.

Chapter 3
Since the fall of man in the Garden of Eden, God has been working to restore man back to his original condition and position. God created Adam in His own image, an image bearer of God, in His likeness and with His nature.

Chapter 4

REDEMPTION, RESTORATION AND
RECONCILIATION

Preaching the Good News is not the only commission for God's royal priesthood of believers. Christians are also called to demonstrate the ministry of reconciliation. We accomplish this charge by using Jesus' name to overcome those things in the earth that are out of harmony with His Kingdom.

Chapter 5

THE GENESIS MANDATE

God blessed man with the ability to govern the earth and establish the Kingdom of God. We are kingly stewards of His creation. From five blessings, what I call the Genesis Mandate, we get a tremendous understanding of God's greatness toward Adam and Eve.

Chapter 6

THE KINGDOM AND WORLD SYSTEMS

Every kingdom of this world that we invade with the Gospel of the Kingdom will require a spiritual fight with demonic governing authorities. Scripture offers clear instructions on overcoming the kingdoms of this world: "Submit yourselves therefore to God, resist the devil and he will flee" (James 4:7).

Chapter 7

THE SON OF MAN

The born again believer has been endowed with a "delegated

sovereignty" both natural and spiritual. As the clash of kingdoms continues we can choose to respond in a number of ways. We can surrender, withdraw, compromise, be indifferent – or become Kingdom reformers.

Jesus confirmed His Kingship when He healed the sick, cast out devils, provided food supernaturally, and rebuked death, wind, storm and sea. He said repeatedly when demonstrating His Kingship, "The Kingdom of heaven has come unto you."

A person who cannot change his thinking cannot change his life. Thoughts shape your life. To enter kingship we must learn to think like kings and then we will act like kings. Kings hold the keys to authority.

A revolutionist insists on a different way of thinking and living – a change. Jesus' revolution is one of righteousness. It confronts opposing forces wherever they appear. His revolution is found in the establishing of the Kingdom of God on the earth and He wants to use you as a 21st century revolutionary.

Chapter 11

WORLD CHANGERS & HISTORY MAKERS 159
The Gospel of the Kingdom is the only true gospel. It boldly proclaims that the Kingdom of God has come to the earth. It offers the Good News that, through repentance of sin, we can be restored to our kingship as believers and launched into this world with a dominion agenda. We were not created for heaven but for earth.

Chapter 12

KINGSHIP: A FORWARD SHIFT 175
We can no longer sit idly by watching our world sink into moral decay. The Church is called to lead change and reform in our nation and throughout the earth. The Kingdom of God is not a future event. The Kingdom of God is here and now.

INTRODUCTION

What if I told you that you are a king? You have a domain. You have authority. And you have inbuilt power to live in victory over financial setbacks, health hurdles, relationship conflicts, and every other circumstance that doesn't agree with God's will for your life? Well, that's exactly what I am telling you. Actually, the Apostle Peter said it best when the Holy Spirit inspired him to write: "Ye are a chosen generation, a royal priesthood, an holy nation, a peculiar people..." (1 Peter 2:9) In modern English, that means you are a king!

Indeed, when you accepted Jesus Christ as your King and Lord you did more than secure your salvation. You also became a king in the Kingdom of Light – a king with a purpose, anointing, and destiny. Now it's up to you to live that royal life. It's up to you to be fruitful, to multiply, to replenish, to subdue and to take dominion in the earth according to the biblical pattern. And you possess the God-given abilities to do just that.

Listen, God didn't save you so just so you could have assurance that you will go to heaven one day. No, God has a unique plan for your life. He really does. He wants to use you in ways you may never have dreamed were possible. But before you can fully manifest Kingdom promises in your life you have to know who you are and what belongs to you as one of Christ's kings. And you have to submit your authority to His plan to establish the Kingdom of God in earth.

Doubtless, as you begin to see yourself as a king, you will walk in new levels of spiritual authority, prosperity, and dominion – all for the glory of God. Kingdom Living offers you keys that will help you renew your mind and strengthen your spirit so you can fulfill your destiny in Christ. So get ready to discover new levels of the believer's authority and your kingship. You'll be glad you did.

Your Partner,

Jonas Clark

Chapter 1

REVEALING YOUR KINGSHIP

Many believers have a difficult time thinking of themselves as kings. For some, suggesting that believers adopt a kingship mentality meets with resistance because it launches negative concepts of unwarranted superiority, abuse of authority, unearned respect, and even an uppity attitude. None of these images, however, convey the intended biblical concept of kingship.

What is your reason for being? Have you ever considered what matters most in your life? Every believer is qualified as a member of a kingly priesthood and called to demonstrate the praises of

Him who has called them out of spiritual darkness, blindness and ignorance (1 Peter 2:9). But how do believers walk worthy of that call? They do it by sharing the salvation message: Jesus died for our sins and offers reconciliation (return to favor) through His atoning blood for those who repent of their sin.

Sharing the Gospel of salvation, however, is not where the ministry of the believer's kingly priesthood ends. Rather, it is only the beginning. Jesus also wants us to advance and establish the Kingdom of God. Jesus taught us to pray, "Thy kingdom come, thy will be done, as in heaven, so in earth" (Luke 11:2). It is apparent from this Scripture that the Lord wants His Kingdom and will to impact the earth through His sons and daughters.

CONCEPT OF RESTORATION

Since the fall of Adam God has been working to restore this world back to Himself. In fact, the Word of God proclaims a restitution (Greek *apokatastasis*) of all things. Scripture declares,

> "Repent ye therefore, and be converted, that your sins may be blotted out, when the times of refreshing shall come from the presence of the Lord; And he shall send Jesus Christ,

which before was preached unto you: Who the heaven must receive until the times of restitution of all things, which God hath spoken by the mouth of all his holy prophets since the world began" (Acts 3:19-21).

We will be exploring the secrets of this pivotal verse throughout this book.

The English word restitution means "the act of restoring to the rightful owner something that has been taken away, lost, or stolen." The Greek word *apokatastasis* means "to return this earth back to its perfect state before the fall."

In keeping with that restoration, there has been a return of modern day apostles and apostolic functions to the Body of Christ and His Church. Not just in apostolic titles but more importantly in function. Mature believers are savvy enough to discern the difference. We need not be fearful of the use of titles because they are nothing more than a description of function.

Since this modern restoration of apostolic grace, several truths are being restored and are coming to the forefront of the Church. We are beginning now to understand that local church structures that rely on the one-man-only model and pastor-does-all view of ministry are ineffective. We are learning that every equipped joint (believer) actually supplies something for the "increase of the body" (Ephesians 4:16). At the same time, we are also seeing the apostolic grace usher in a fresh focus on reaching the lost and taking the Gospel of the Kingdom into all nations. And, of course, there is an emerging interest in taking dominion in the marketplace in what some are calling the Marketplace Movement.

The restoration of these truths and adoption of these mindsets is part and parcel of Jesus' restoration ministry. In other words, apostolic grace and a dominion mindset are part of what Jesus is restoring. It is one more step in His mission to restore all things back to their original state. Scripture says,

> "And, having made peace through the blood of his cross, by him to reconcile (Greek *apokatallasso*) all things unto himself; by him, I say, whether they be things in earth, or things in heaven" (Colossians 1:20).

Every believer, therefore, is called to continue the restoration ministry of Jesus – to return all things back to the former state of harmony. Throughout this book we will discover many of the "things" Jesus is restoring, particularly the kingship position of the born again believer. Jesus revealed to us the pattern of restoration in this Scripture,

"What man shall there be among you, that shall have one sheep, and if it fall into a pit on the Sabbath day, will he not lay hold on it, and lift it out? How much then is a man better than a sheep? Wherefore it is lawful to do well on the Sabbath days. Then saith he to the man, 'Stretch forth thine hand.' And he stretched it forth; and it was restored (*apokathistemi*) whole, like as the other" (Matthew 12:10-13).

Patterns lead to a final product. Jesus' pattern for restoration will lead to a glorious Church without spot or wrinkle. One day it will be evident "The kingdoms of this world are become the kingdoms of our Lord, and of his Christ; and he shall reign for ever and ever" (Revelation 11:15). That day will come after the restoration of all things is complete. In the meantime, it's time for the royal priesthood to wake up and get busy.

KING OF KINGS

How many times have you heard, "Jesus is King of kings and Lord of lords?" I suspect you have heard this many times throughout your Christian walk. But what is significant about that statement? Is it simply another title for Jesus or can we learn something more by exploring this designation more thoroughly?

We believers in Jesus Christ have no problem understanding that Jesus is the King. After all, that is His title and position. We even refer to Jesus as the King of the Universe. There are many Scriptures that teach Jesus is the King of kings including:

- "And he hath on his vesture and on his thigh a name written, King of kings, and Lord of lords" (Revelation 19:16). Lord of lords literally means Ruler of rulers.

- "Which in his times he shall show, who is the blessed and only Potentate, the King of kings, and Lord of lords" (1 Timothy 6:15).

- "These shall make war with the Lamb, and the Lamb shall overcome them: for he is Lord of lords, and King of kings: and they that are with him are called, and chosen, and faithful" (Revelation 17:4).

Notice all of these Scriptures use the statement "King of kings." This brings up an important question, "Who are the kings that Jesus is the King of?"

WHO ARE THE KINGS?

There was a time when I didn't give this question much thought. When I did, I assumed it was referring to the kings of Old Testament times, like David or Solomon. Yes, He was the King of those kings, but that's not the whole answer. You and I – born again believers – are the kings of New Testament times. Better said, Jesus is the King of *us* kings. "So what does this mean to me?" you ask. That's what this study is all about. My prayer is that every chapter will bring you closer to the answer, your role, rights and privileges as kings in the Kingdom of God.

I suspect that many who hear the statement that Jesus is the King of kings automatically focus in on Jesus' role as King. I submit to you that this declaration has an important reference to you, too. Could it be possible that the Lord wants us to know something more about ourselves and our position in Christ? Before we dig in to the unfolding mystery of the kingship of every believer and the Kingdom of God, let's first take a look at the priesthood of every believer because this is what's most familiar to us.

A PRIESTHOOD OF KINGS

Christians, for the most part, have an understanding of their ministry as priests. They sing, worship, praise, preach, pray, and teach the Word of God to others. Scripture says,

> "Ye also, as lively stones, are built up a spiritual house, an holy priesthood, to offer up spiritual sacrifices, acceptable to God by Jesus Christ" (1 Peter 2:5).

Since the Great Protestant Reformation of the 1500s believers have come to understand "by grace are you saved through faith and not of yourselves it is the gift of God" (Ephesians 2:8). This truth paved the way for the restoration of every believer's priesthood.

The Apostle Peter described the ministry of the priesthood of every believer. He said that the priest's duties were to offer up "spiritual sacrifices" to God. In fact, the very life of a born again believer is a "spiritual house" charged with offering up praise, prayer, thanksgiving, and living a lifestyle of overcoming faith and victory. But then Peter added something that may seem a bit odd, yet, very important; he said that the believers are a royal priesthood.

"But ye are a chosen generation, <u>a royal priesthood,</u> an holy nation, a peculiar people; that ye should show forth the praises of him who hath called you out of darkness into his marvelous light" (1 Peter 2:9; emphasis added).

Notice the statement "royal priesthood," especially the word "royal." Royal is the Greek word *basileios* meaning "regal" or "kingly." I am going to bring this word up throughout this teaching, so it is important to remember it. This Scripture teaches us that we, as believers, are part of a kingly, even regal priesthood of believers.

> Not only are you a priest, you are part of a priesthood of kings – you are royalty!

Better said, a priesthood of kings. Are you getting it yet?

Not only are you a priest, you are part of a priesthood of kings – you are royalty!

REGAL BELIEVERS

With that said, we need to see ourselves as both priests and kings of the Lord Jesus Christ. We seem to grasp and agree with the concept of a priesthood of believers, but to think of ourselves as kings, that's quite another story. Christians don't have a problem with praying, singing, worshipping, or praising God, but to see themselves as actual kings seems a bit difficult to grasp.

Many believers have a hard time thinking of themselves as kings. For some, suggesting that believers adopt a kingship mentality meets with resistance because it launches negative concepts of unwarranted superiority, abuse of authority, unearned respect, and even an uppity attitude. None of these images, however, convey the intended biblical concept of kingship. As born again people we understand our calling to humble ourselves under the mighty hand of God, serving one another in love, and not being a respecter of persons. In fact, we recognize the greatest in the Kingdom of God is the servant of all (Mark 10:44). So, what does it mean, then, to be one of the kings that Jesus is King of?

AS IN HEAVEN, SO IN EARTH

Let's look at the Word of God for a moment. Jesus taught His disciples,

> "When ye pray, say, our Father which art in heaven, hallowed be thy name, thy kingdom come, thy will be done, as in heaven, so in

earth. Give us day by day our daily bread..."
(Luke 11:2-3).

Notice the word "Kingdom" in this verse. It is the Greek word *basileia* meaning "royal power, dominion, rule and kingship." Jesus literally told His disciples to pray for His Kingdom to manifest on earth and His will to be done on earth just as it is in heaven.

In order for God's will to be done on earth it must be done through His people. God is a Spirit. He wants His Body, the Body of Christ, to positively impact this earth. As the Body of Christ we have the ability, *and* the responsibility, to produce His will on earth through a lifestyle of prayer and action. Not only are we His Body, we are also His priesthood of kings and we have been entrusted as stewards over His creation. Jesus commanded, "Occupy till I come" (Luke 19:13). In order to occupy for Jesus, we need to stand in our role as kings and learn how to activate our spiritual authority to advance and establish the Kingdom of God on earth.

ACTION STEPS

Here are two things you can do to discover your kingship.

First, recognize that you are one of Jesus' kings. Think of the possibilities. Start seeing yourself as one with spiritual authority, a regal believer. Remember when you used to doodle on scraps of paper in school? Now take a minute and draw a crown. Imagine what it would be like to put that crown on your head. After all, kings do wear crowns. Kingship is biblical. The Bible says we will cast our crowns at Jesus' feet. You are a king. You have a crown. It's OK to put it on.

Second, for the next seven days pray Luke 11:2-4. Make the prayer personal, "<u>My Father</u> which art in heaven, hallowed by thy name, thy kingdom come <u>in my life</u>, thy will be done in my life, as in heaven so in earth. <u>Give me this day</u> my daily bread and forgive me of my sins, for <u>I also forgive</u> every one that sins against me. <u>And lead me</u> not into temptation; but <u>deliver me</u> from evil."

Did you know that Jesus trained the most effective revolutionary leadership team of all time? In the next chapter we will go back to those 40 days before Jesus ascended into the heavens and examine His teaching on the Kingdom.

APERÇU

Jesus is King of kings and Lord of lords.

Priests offer up "spiritual sacrifices" acceptable to God (1 Peter 2:5).

Believers are part of a royal priesthood (1 Peter 2:9).

Royal is the Greek word *basileios* meaning "regal or kingly."

Many believers have a hard time thinking of themselves as kings. For some, suggesting that believers adopt a kingship mentality meets with resistance because it launches negative concepts of unwarranted superiority, abuse of authority, unearned respect, and even an uppity attitude. None of these images, however, convey the intended biblical concept of kingship.

Jesus taught His disciples to pray "thy kingdom come, thy will be done, as in heaven, so in earth" (Luke 11:2-3).

Chapter 2

JESUS' 40-DAY
KINGSHIP SEMINAR

*After Jesus was resurrected, He spent the last 40 days of His
earthy ministry talking to His disciples about the Kingdom
of God. The emphasis that Jesus placed on imparting the
fullness of the Kingdom revelation gives us insight into how
important Jesus deemed it to the restoration of all things.*

Kings quest progress. Imagine for a moment that
Jesus, your triumphant King, has just been
resurrected. He has demonstrated His power over
death and holds the keys to death, hell and the grave. He
has invited you to a 40-day seminar. You are gathered
with other disciples with a unique opportunity to

listen to Jesus' final teachings right before He departs into heaven. Doubtless, these are some of the most important instructions Jesus will ever give His team of revolutionaries. Think about it. Jesus was about to leave this earth and leave His Gospel of the Kingdom to those that remained in the world. We cannot for a moment underestimate the magnitude of this meeting. Let's listen in. Scripture says,

> "To whom also he showed himself alive after his passion by many infallible proofs, being seen of them forty days, and speaking of the things pertaining to the kingdom of God" (Acts 1:3).

> Jesus spent so much time teaching about the Kingdom and restoration throughout His ministry that the disciples thought the restoration of the Kingdom was imminent.

So we see that the subject of the meetings was the Kingdom (Greek *basileia*) of God.

The Greek word *basileia* (kingdom) translates as "Kingdom of God" 70 times and "Kingdom of Heaven" 33 times in the King James Version of the New Testament. (See appendix for complete list.) The statement "the kingdom" occurs in 126 verses. Jesus had a lot to say about the Kingdom. The four strongest definitions of the Greek word *basileia* (kingdom) are:

1. Royal Power

2. Kingship

3. Dominion

4. Rule

A TIMELY TOPIC

After Jesus was resurrected, He spent the last 40 days of His earthy ministry talking to His disciples about the Kingdom of God. The emphasis that Jesus placed on imparting the fullness of the Kingdom revelation gives us insight into how important Jesus deemed it to the restoration of all things. We know that Jesus talked a great deal about kingship and restoration because after the meetings were over, those in attendance asked him:

> "Lord, wilt thou at this time restore again the kingdom to Israel?" (Acts 1:6)

Jesus spent so much time teaching about the Kingdom and restoration throughout His ministry that the disciples thought the restoration of the Kingdom was imminent.

   + The word "restore" in Greek is *apokathistemi* meaning "to restore to a former state of harmony."

With this said we can easily conclude that Jesus taught a 40-day seminar built around the theme of kingship (*basileia*), including the restitution of all things. We will explore that same theme throughout this work.

We should be careful not to focus exclusively on the restoration of Israel. If we do we will miss some extremely important truths. Confusing the Kingship of Christ with the restoration of Israel only is still prevalent today. Of course, Israel is included in the *apokathistemi* (restoration) plan of God, yet the Kingship of Christ is not limited to the nation of Israel. We are going to discover that the restoration that Jesus taught His disciples encompassed the entire earth and directly affects your life.

In summing up the all-important 40-day seminar, Jesus commanded His future world-changing reformers to go into Jerusalem and wait for the promise of the Father, the baptism of the Holy Spirit (Acts 1:4, 8).

THE KINGSHIP PREREQUISITE

Untold myriads of sermons have been preached on the subject of the baptism of the Holy Spirit, yet I wonder if we can really grasp why Jesus considered it so vital. Is it possible that the restitution of all things, the kingship restoration message, can never be accomplished without the assistance of the Holy Spirit Himself?

Jesus had spoken of this same promise once before, when He said,

> "If you love me, keep my commandments. And I will pray the Father, and he shall give you another Comforter, that he may abide with you forever, even the Spirit of truth; whom the world cannot receive, because it seeth him not, neither knoweth him: but you know him; for he dwelleth with you, and shall be in you" (John 14:15-17).

Jesus also declared,

> "For John truly baptized with water; but you shall be baptized with the Holy Ghost not many days hence." Jesus further told them that they would "receive power after that the Holy Ghost was come upon them and that they would be witnesses unto him" (Acts 1:4-8).

John the Baptist foretold of this great event prophesying,

> "I indeed baptize you with water unto repentance: but he that cometh after me is mightier than I, whose shoes I am not worthy to bear: he shall baptize you with the Holy Ghost and with fire" (Matthew 3:11).

When Jesus talked about the Kingdom of God, was He only referring to salvation? Could there be far more to His message than that? Could He have been discoursing about an even broader topic? Could the Kingdom of God message include the restoration of all things, kingship of the believer and Christ's dominion? Could it be possible that the baptism of the Holy Spirit was a prerequisite for His followers to experience both their priesthood and kingship blessings?

What we do know is this. It doesn't take a 40-day seminar to talk about the importance of man's salvation. Surely Jesus was teaching on something deeper that the simple message of salvation. Indeed, it is clear that Jesus was talking about:

1. Kingship of every believer

2. Restoration of all things

3. Advancement and establishing of
the Kingdom of God on the earth

THE HIDDEN KINGDOM

Jesus' seminar was not the first time the disciples were taught about His plan to establish the Kingdom of God. Scripture says,

> "And he sent them to preach the Kingdom of God, and to heal the sick" (Luke 9:2; emphasis added).

But what does that mean? If you asked 20 people today what it means to preach the Kingdom of God I suspect you would get 20 different answers. Could it be possible that we have lost the definition? Could it be possible that something happened in the early Church that distracted us from the true meaning of preaching the Kingdom of God? Has the timeline of history stolen some truth from us? Is there a hidden kingship message somewhere in Scripture to be found that would clear this up?

Again, I am convinced that Jesus talked about more than the salvation message during His final meeting with His disciples on earth because they asked Him this question at the end of the seminar,

"Lord, will thou at this time restore again the kingdom to Israel?" (Acts 1:6)

That question makes it clear that most of the subject matter of the meeting was about kingship, the Kingdom of God, and the restoration of all things. The question today is: What happened to the message Jesus taught during those 40 days? Why have we not heard more about our kingship role in the restitution of all things?

RELIGIOUS OPPOSITION

If kingship, the Kingdom, and the restoration of all things was the message the early apostles were commanded to preach then what happened to it? Could it be that religious legalism in the early Church changed the focus of the Gospel of the Kingdom? Could it be that the *religious spirit* began to oppose the reconciliation of all things and the kingship of every believer through legalistic prejudice? Could it be that religious opposition to the kingship message has affected us even today? I believe the answer to all of those questions is "yes."

When the Apostle Paul preached the Gospel of Jesus Christ to the Gentiles, thousands were born again. This so infuriated many Jews from the Church in Jerusalem that a great controversy ensued. The issue that brought such tumult was circumcision. Many felt it was impossible for a Gentile to be born again without keeping the Law of Moses, which required circumcision.

Notice the focus of the religious Christians was on an outward legalistic issue instead of the inward condition of the heart. I was amazed the day I realized that it was "born again" Jews from Jerusalem, Judaizers, that were following the Apostle Paul to oppose his ministry to the Gentiles. Legalists have always blocked the Gospel of the Kingdom. They still do today. Legalism in the early Church took the focus off of the Kingship of Christ through His sons and daughters and placed it on the "letter of the law."

RELIGIOUS LEGALISM

Jesus warned that religious spirits were dangerous because they blocked the entrance to the kingship of heaven for men,

"But woe unto you, scribes and Pharisees, hypocrites! For ye shut up the kingdom of heaven against men: for ye neither go in yourselves, neither suffer ye them that are entering to go in" (Matthew 23:13).

Could it be possible that Jesus was not simply referring to salvation but something more? Fighting over circumcision was only the first in a long battle of legalistic issues the Church has faced over the last 2,000 years. We may not be arguing over circumcision today, but there are plenty of other legalistic matters Christians take issue against. The bottom line is religious legalism is still deterring our focus on demonstrating the kingship of our Christ as seen through the active faith of every born again believer. In my book "*30 Pieces of Silver*" you can find successful strategies to overcome religious opposition to your kingship authority.

Is it possible that the religious spirit, legalism, self-righteousness, and hypocrisy, stopped the preaching of the Gospel of the Kingdom? Let's take a closer look.

Assume for a minute that the religious spirit could steal the kingship-of-every-believer message. What would be the most effective way to accomplish that sinister goal? One possible way would be to teach a non-biblical separation of clergy and laity. Is it possible that the kingship teaching was hijacked by religious terrorists and antichrist spirits that infiltrated the early Church? I submit to you that it is quite possible and even probable. (See 1 John 2:18-19; Philippians 2:20-21).

The early Church is rightly portrayed as abundant in signs, wonders, and miracles. But it was also the stage for unmitigated heresy, lawlessness, and rebellion. We know that there were, for example, teachers that opposed justification by faith. We also know that these teachers demanded that people keep the ceremonial laws of the Old Testament. Some taught that the resurrection from the dead had already taken place (2 Timothy 2:18). Some even taught that the resurrection could never happen (1 Corinthians 15:12). The worship of angels was also promoted (Colossians 2:8, 18-23, 1 Timothy 4:1-3). Amid all of these false teachings, it is evident that the kingship message and the restoration of all things faced major opposition in the early Church.

RELIGION'S HEY-DAY: THE DARK AGES

One only needs to study the council of Nicene in 326 A.D. to discover that the priesthood and kingship of every believer was robbed from the lay Christian and handed over to an elite group of bishops. At this tipping-point meeting it was determined that the ordinary believer could not take an active role in ministry. Granted, this meeting was about protecting the Church from heresy but the result was the beginning of the institutionalized Church. That was only the first of religion's attack on the believer's Spirit-led liberty. To further the separation between ministry function and the believer's royal priesthood, Pope Leo the First declared himself to be the Infallible Vicar of Christ in 400 A.D. This was nothing less than the continuation of Roman emperor worship shrouded in pseudo-Christianity. These acts propelled the Church into a time of spiritual free fall known as the Dark Ages. Out of this chaos emerged a religious Church that battled against anyone who tried to rise into the believer's place of spiritual authority (Revelation 17:5). It seems that the 40-day kingship message was lost during these dark times. Or was it a planted seed waiting to come up in our generation?

ACTION STEPS

Here are two keys that will help you understand the Kingdom of God teachings on which Jesus focused during His last 40 days on earth.

First, Jesus concentrated His teaching ministry on the subject of the Kingdom of God. This week read each Scripture that includes the key phrases, "Kingdom of God" or "Kingdom of Heaven." (You can find a list of these Scriptures in the appendix of this book.) As you meditate on these Scriptures, continually keep in mind that Jesus promised, "The Father is well pleased to give unto you the Kingdom."

Second, the baptism of the Holy Spirit with the evidence of speaking in other tongues is vital to your kingship. Remember that Jesus told His disciples to "wait for the promise" before they set out to advance and establish the Kingdom of God in their lives and ministries. If the baptism of the Holy Spirit was important for them, then it is equally important for you.

What if you could find out why you were born? How would that affect your life? Would you conduct yourself differently? In the next chapter we are going to look at God's original blueprint for you. He's the Master Builder, your Creator. Let's see how He designed you as you search for your purpose in Him.

APERÇU

The Greek word *basileia* (kingdom) translates as "kingdom of God" 70 times and "kingdom of heaven" 33 times in the King James Version of the New Testament.

The four strongest definitions of the Greek word *basileia* (kingdom) are royal power, kingship, dominion, and rule.

The word "restore" in Greek is *apokathistemi* meaning "to restore to a former state of harmony."

Israel is included in the *apokathistemi* (restoration) plan of God, yet the Kingship of Christ is not limited to the nation of Israel.

Legalism in the early Church took the focus off of the Kingship of Christ through His sons and daughters and placed it on the "letter of the law."

The early Church is rightly portrayed as abundant in signs, wonders, and miracles. But it was also the stage for unmitigated heresy, lawlessness, and rebellion.

The council of Nicene in 326 A.D. robbed every believer of their priesthood and kingship.

Chapter 3

KINGSHIP: THE ORIGINAL INTENT

Since the fall of man in the Garden of Eden, God has been working to restore man back to his original condition and position. God created Adam in His own image, an image bearer of God, in His likeness and with His nature.

K ingship was God's original intent – and He hasn't changed His mind. From the moment Adam lost his kingship and was expelled from the Garden of Eden God has been working all things after the counsel of

His will – to restore this world and everything in it back to Himself. Luke records God's plan,

> "Repent ye therefore, and be converted, that your sins may be blotted out, when the times of refreshing shall come from the presence of the Lord; And he shall send Jesus Christ, which before was preached unto you: Who the heaven must receive until the times of restitution of all things, which God hath spoken by the mouth of all his holy prophets since the world began" (Acts 3:19-21).

Restoration is the act of restoring to the rightful owner something that has been taken away, lost, or stolen. The word "restitution" in this Scripture comes from the Greek word *apokatastasis*, meaning "to return this earth back to its perfect state of harmony before the fall."

GOD'S IMAGE BEARER

Since the fall of man in the Garden of Eden, God has been working to restore (*apokatastasis*) man back to his original condition and position. In the beginning, we know that God created Adam in His own image, in His likeness and with His nature (Genesis 1:26). The Word says that "God formed man from the dust of the ground and breathed life (not air) into his nostrils and man became a living soul with identity and purpose – to fellowship with God and have dominion over this earth (Genesis 1:26; 2:7).

In the original creation Adam was perfect. He lived out of his spirit. He communed with God out of his spirit. He was connected to God through his spirit. He named the animals from his spirit. He tended the garden from his spirit. He exercised his kingship, or dominion, over the earth out of his spirit.

Scripture tells us that God put Adam in the Garden of Eden to dress it and to keep it. He also gave Adam a command:

> "Of every tree of the garden thou mayest freely eat: But of the tree of the knowledge of good and evil, thou shalt not eat of it: for in the day that thou eatest thereof thou shalt surely die" (Genesis 2:17).

Of course, Adam did not immediately die when he ate of the fruit. He lived to be 930 years old. God was talking about a spiritual death.

Some time after this we read the testimony of Eve's deception by the serpent. That old serpent told Eve that the reason God didn't want her to eat of the tree of the knowledge of good and evil was because her eyes would be opened and she would be like

God (Genesis 3:5). The reality was that Adam and Eve were already like God. They were created with the very nature of God, in the image of God, blessed by God, and given dominion over the earth by God.

THE GREAT DISCONNECT

We all know the sad conclusion. Eve partook and Adam did, too. Sin entered the earth and Adam's spirit died because the wages of sin is death (Romans 6:23). Adam's disobedience caused a communal disconnect between his spirit and the Spirit of God. Adam and Eve began to live out of their souls instead of their spirits. (Your soul is your mind, will, intellect, reasoning, imagination and emotion.) They were led by their five senses – touch, hearing, sight, smell and taste – instead of their spirits. Before the fall they simply knew what they needed to know. They could draw any knowledge they needed directly from God's Spirit. Their fall marked the genesis of education by intellect and reasoning rather than spirit and revelation.

When God came into the garden to fellowship with Adam, he heard the Lord's voice and tried to hide among the trees. God called out to Adam, asking "Where art thou?" Adam replied, "I heard thy voice in the garden, and I was afraid because I was naked; and I hid myself" (Genesis 2:8-10). Of course, God knew where Adam was all along. God is all-knowing. He didn't ask because He didn't know.

God knew where Adam was physically but He couldn't find Adam in His Spirit. For the first time Adam was not connected to God through his spirit. Adam's spirit was dead.

From that moment on, God determined to restore mankind back to Himself. I can almost hear God saying, "Adam, I know what it will take to restore you and I'm coming to get you." In order to work this out to the counsel of His will, God had to send the Second Adam, the Lord Jesus Christ, the Lamb of God that taketh away the sin of the world (1 Corinthians 15:45). The only way for a man's spirit to live again is by being born again. Jesus said,

"Except a man be born again he cannot see the kingdom of God" (John 3:3).

For a man to be born again he must repent of his sins, ask Jesus to cleanse him from all unrighteousness, and make Jesus Lord of his life.

MAN'S GREAT DECEPTION

The great deception that the Serpent posed to Eve was "you will be like God." The reality was that Adam and

Eve were already like God. They were created with the very nature of God, bearers of the very image of God, blessed by God, and given dominion over the earth by God. Yet Adam was not satisfied submitting his kingship to the one that made him a king. Adam wanted to be self-governed.

What we need to understand here is that Adam didn't fall from heaven. He fell from grace. His sin disconnected him from heaven, which was in another realm in the very garden he was still standing. Our ultimate destination as born again believers is not heaven, but earth. Could it be possible that heaven is all around us in an unseen dimension that Jesus called the Kingdom? Even a rapture will only take us to heaven for a short time. We will eventually return to this earth to rule and reign with Christ. We don't need incorruptible resurrected bodies to live in heaven. We need them for life on earth. Scripture makes it clear that heaven belongs to God and the earth belongs to man,

> Could it be possible that heaven is all around us in an unseen dimension that Jesus called the Kingdom?

"The heaven, even the heavens, are the Lord's: but the earth hath he given to the children of men" (Psalm 115:16).

KINGSHIP DESIGNED

Today mankind struggles for identity, purpose and direction. Not understanding our purpose is the foundation for all failure. God's original intent for man has always been to fellowship with Him. We were designed from the beginning to take dominion over this earth that God has created.

Let's examine some of the things He had in mind.

1. God created man to love.

2. God created man to share His creation.

3. God created man for fellowship.

4. God created man because He wanted a family.

5. God created man to rule with Him over creation.

6. God created man to demonstrate His magnificence to the heavenly host.

7. God created man, a free will being, to worship Him.

A SPIRIT-LED LIFE

We were designed from the beginning to take dominion over this earth that God has created. We can never get back to that place of original intent, kingship submitted to Christ the King, until we are first born again, submitted to His Word, and subsequently learn to live out of our born again spirits. It's our born again spirit that connects us to the Kingdom of Heaven. Scripture says that the Holy Spirit is our teacher who will lead us and guide us in all truth (John 16:13). He is the one that is actively involved in the restitution of all things.

Friend, the Spirit-led life "is" the answer to walking out your kingship. The Apostle Peter said we are a priesthood of kings (1 Peter 2:9). Jesus said it is the Father's good pleasure to give us the Kingdom (Luke 12:32). Scripture declares that all creation is waiting for the manifestation of the sons of God (Romans 8:19). How can we manifest as sons? By exercising our kingship authority as believers and walking out the restored biblical truths of our generation.

THE SEED HAS BEEN PLANTED

Every "movement" throughout history has resulted in some form of truth being restored to the Body of

Christ that led to more glory being given to Christ and the further establishing of the Kingdom of God. After the resurrection of Jesus, religious spirits attacked the Church and we plunged into the Dark Ages. Yet the "seed of the Kingdom of God" had already been planted and was destined to outgrow everything (Mark 4:31). The greatest opposition to the restoration of kingship is the spirit of religion.

> "For the kingdom of God is not meat and drink (*legalism and religion*); but righteousness, and peace, and joy in the Holy Ghost" (Romans 14:17).

Consider this: It took over 2,000 years for the Church to be prepared for the restoration of this kingship of every believer truth. God's original intent for you was to be His image bearer. He created you for regal status. We are in the times of restitution and He will not leave you out.

ACTION STEPS

Kingship is God's original intent for you and you can have a Spirit-led walk with Christ. Start developing your spirit today. You can do so by meditating on the Scriptures. Contemplation or musing on a subject or particular verse is a powerful tool in releasing deep truths within you. I like the Apostle Paul's prayer,

> "I cease not to give thanks for you, making mention of you in my prayers: That the God of our Lord Jesus Christ, the Father of glory, may give unto you the spirit of wisdom and revelation in the knowledge of him. The eyes of your understanding being enlightened; that you may know what is the hope of his calling and what the riches of the glory of his inheritance in the saints, And what is the exceeding greatness of his power to us-ward who believe, according to the working of his mighty power" (Ephesians 1:16-19).

Next, find a good strong local church and plug yourself in. Living stones hang out together.

In the next chapter we will look at two vital aspects of Jesus' ministry– restoration and redemption – and how you are directly involved in establishing the Kingdom of God.

APERÇU

Since the fall of Adam God has been working to restore this world back to Himself.

The English word *restitution* means "the act of restoring to the rightful owner something that has been taken away, lost, or stolen."

God created Adam in His own image, an image bearer of God, in His likeness and with His nature (Genesis 1:26).

Adam was "connected" to God, spirit to Spirit.

The fall was the genesis of education through the soul. Man's insatiable hunger for knowledge is the result of the fall. Before the fall they simply knew what they needed to know.

The great deception that the Serpent posed to Eve was "you will be like God." The reality was that Adam and Eve were already like God.

Adam was not satisfied submitting his kingship to the one that made him a king. Adam wanted to be self-governed.

The foundation for all failure is rooted in a lack of understanding our purpose in life, how God designed us and what we are called to do.

We can never get back to that place of original intent, kingship submitted to Christ the King, until we are first born again, submitted to His Word, and subsequently learn to live out of our born again spirits.

The Spirit-led life "is" the answer to finding and walking out your kingship authority (Romans 8:14).

The greatest opposition to the restoration of kingship is the spirit of religion.

Chapter 4

REDEMPTION, RESTORATION & RECONCILIATION

Preaching the Good News is not the only commission for God's royal priesthood of believers. Christians are also called to demonstrate the ministry of reconciliation. We accomplish this charge by using Jesus' name to overcome those things in the earth that are out of harmony with His Kingdom.

I once thought Jesus had one ministry: to come as the Lamb of God that taketh away the sin of the world. In the early days of my walk with Christ it never occurred to me that Jesus did anything more than offer salvation to men. History proves that I was not alone in my misguided thinking. I now understand the reality that Jesus had more than one ministry. Jesus had the ministry of the Lamb of God *and* the ministry of reconciliation. We can't grab one and ignore the other. Both are extremely important. This understanding will reveal two fundamental truths:

1. The ministry of the Lamb of God deals with the redemption of sinners.

2. The ministry of reconciliation deals with the restoration of all things.

Just as we can participate in the ministry of the Lamb of God through salvation, we can also participate in the reconciliation of all things by exercising our kingship authority. Let's examine the premise.

RETURNED TO FAVOR

Most people understand the concept of reconciliation as it relates to getting born again. Scripture says,

> "And all things are of God, who hath reconciled us to himself by Jesus Christ, and

hath given to us the ministry of reconciliation"
(2 Corinthians 5:18).

Reconciliation (Greek *katallage*) in this verse
signifies "a return to favor." Understanding this, let's
look at the manifestation of this reconciliation after
the baptism of the Holy Spirit in the Upper Room.
The disciples asked Jesus, "Lord, wilt thou at this time
restore (*apokathistemi*) again the kingdom (*basileia*) to
Israel?" (Acts 1:6) Again, this question was posed after
hearing Jesus teach about the "Kingdom of God" for 40
days (Acts 1:3). Jesus concluded His teaching series by
telling them to wait for the baptism of the Holy Spirit.
We all know what happened in Acts 2. The Holy Spirit
fell on those assembled in the Upper Room and filled
them with dunamis power. Now they were ready to
engage the world with the Gospel of the Kingdom.

PETER'S BOLD DECLARATION

After they were baptized with the Holy Spirit, the
disciples left the Upper Room and hit the streets.
Many people accused them of being drunk because
of the way they were acting. Obviously there was
something visually different about them. They
thought only drunk people could be so happy. Peter

described what happened to them in his famous "This Is That" sermon.

> "But Peter, standing up with the eleven, lifted up his voice, and said unto them, Ye men of Judea, and all ye that dwell at Jerusalem, be this known unto you, and hearken to my words: For these are not drunken, as ye suppose, seeing it is but the third hour of the day. But this is that which was spoken by the prophet Joel; And it shall come to pass in the last days, saith God, I will pour out of my Spirit upon all flesh: and your sons and your daughters shall prophesy, and your young men shall see visions, and your old men shall dream dreams: And on my servants and on my handmaidens I will pour out in those days of my Spirit; and they shall prophesy: And I will show wonders in heaven above, and signs in the earth beneath; blood, and fire, and vapor of smoke: The sun shall be turned into darkness, and the moon into blood, before that great and notable day of the Lord come: And it shall come to pass, that whosoever shall call on the name of the Lord shall be saved" (Acts 2:14-21).

The conclusion of Peter's preaching brought godly repentance to thousands who were subsequently born again. That message was a demonstration of the ministry of reconciliation (*katallage*), because it returned the listeners back to favor with God through repentance of sin and the acceptance of the ministry of the Lamb of God who suffered crucifixion and offered atonement for their sin. This event in the Upper Room is commonly referred to as the birth of the New Testament Church. The born again experience, regeneration through repentance and faith in Christ, is the prerequisite for kingship. Jesus said,

"Verily, verily, I say unto thee, except a man be born again he cannot see the kingdom of God" (John 3:3).

The born again experience is a return to favor with God. Not only do you find favor (reconciliation), you are transported out of the kingdom of darkness into the Kingdom of God. We will discuss this more in another chapter.

RECONCILIATION

For now let's review Jesus' second ministry. This is the same ministry that was later assigned to His disciples, and is now assigned to every born again believer –including you. Kings are reformers. Scripture says,

KINGDOM LIVING: HOW TO ACTIVATE YOUR SPIRITUAL AUTHORITY

"And, having made peace through the blood of
his cross, by him to <u>reconcile</u> all things unto
himself; by him, I say, whether they be things
in earth, or things in heaven" (Colossians 1:20;
emphasis added).

Reconcile here is the Greek word *apokatallasso*
meaning "to bring back to the former state of harmony
before the fall all things." Notice the words "things in
earth" and "things in heaven." This reconciliation wasn't
limited to heaven but encompassed the earth as well.

Apokatallasso is the next type of reconciliation
demonstrated by both Apostles Peter and John. On the
way to prayer Peter and John saw a lame beggar at the
Gate Beautiful. The man, stretching forth his hand in
expectation of receiving alms, met with the solid gaze
of Peter, who commanded,

"Silver and gold have I none: but such as I have
give I thee: In the name of Jesus Christ of
Nazareth rise up and walk" (Acts 3:6).

The man was healed instantly.

That healing encounter was a demonstration of the
second ministry of Jesus: the reconciliation of all things.
Here we see the man's body restored back to its original
design – healthy. Before this incident the lame man's

48   www.JonasClark.com

body was out of harmony with God's original design for his body. His encounter with representatives of Christ resulted in reconciliation.

KINGDOM KEYS

When the Kingdom of God was activated by this lame man's faith, onlookers witnessed a demonstration of the Kingdom of God. Jesus taught His apostles to announce the arrival of the Kingdom of heaven when healing the sick. Jesus said,

> "And as you go, preach, saying, The kingdom of heaven is at hand. Heal the sick, cleanse the lepers, raise the dead, cast out devils: freely ye have received, freely give" (Matthew 10:7-8).

Notice also that the announcement of the Kingdom of heaven was not to signify a future event. When something is "at hand" it is very close to you. It is within reach. It is in your very presence. The Kingdom of God manifested visibly when that which was out of order (harmony) – the man's physical condition – came back into order and in line with God's will. We call that Kingdom restoration. Yes, there is a "now" Kingdom and there is also a future Kingdom.

KINGDOM TODAY AND TOMORROW

George Ladd in his book, *The Gospel of the Kingdom,* [1] explains Kingdom now and Kingdom later like this:

> The Kingdom is a present reality (Matthew 12:28), and yet it is a future blessing (1 Corinthians 15:50). It is an inner spiritual redemptive blessing (Romans 14:17) which can be experienced only by way of the new birth (John 3:3), and yet it will have to do with the government of the nations of the world (Revelation 11:15). The Kingdom is a realm into which men enter now (Matthew 22:32), and yet it is a realm into which they will enter tomorrow (Matthew 8:11). It is at the same time a gift of God which will be bestowed by God in the future (Luke 12:32) and yet which must be received in the present (Mark 10:15). Obviously no simple explanation can do justice to such a rich but diverse variety of teaching.

Clearly the study of the Kingdom of God must be an unfolding mystery that keeps us dependant on the Holy Spirit's continued guidance if we are going to apply the Lordship of Christ in our lives.

God's royal priesthood of believers are not just called to preach the Gospel of salvation. They are also called *to demonstrate the ministry of reconciliation* by using Jesus' name to overcome those things in the earth that are out of harmony with His Kingdom. Jesus said to pray, "Thy kingdom come, thy will be done on earth, just as it is in heaven."

Jesus is King of kings. He has authorized you to carry on His restoration ministry by giving you the "keys of the Kingdom" (Matthew 16:19). Keys unlock doors and represent authority. Jesus has entrusted you with the Gospel message of good news. He has sent you as an ambassador of His Kingdom to preach the acceptable year of the Lord and to advance the restoration of the Kingdom of God by preaching, reforming, and demonstrating restoration and His Kingship. He has given you the keys of the Kingdom and whatever you bind (forbid) on earth is bound in heaven and whatever you loose (allow) on earth is loosed in heaven.

DISCIPLE ALL NATIONS

The Great Commission is not limited to preaching a salvation message to some lost souls. Simply quoting John 3:16 or prancing down the "Roman Road" toward salvation as outlined in Romans Chapter 10 is not fulfilling the biblical mandate that reads,

> "All power is given unto me in heaven and in earth. Go ye therefore, and teach all nations, baptizing them in the name of the Father, and of the Son, and of the Holy Ghost: Teaching them to observe all things whatsoever I have commanded you: and, lo, I am with you always, even unto the end of the world. Amen" (Matthew 28:18-20).

Evangelism, including "teaching them to observe all things," encompasses both the salvation message (Luke 24:47) and the restoration of all things (Matthew 10:7-8).

> God has been in the process of restoring all things back to himself since the fall of Adam.

If we believe that the Gospel of the Kingdom can reconcile a man, what about his family? If the Gospel of the Kingdom can reconcile a family, what about the Church? If the Gospel of the Kingdom can reconcile the Church, what about the nation? Obviously we need to broaden our understanding of the scope of the restoration power in advancing the Gospel of the

Kingdom. Even the honored Jabez understood that and asked God to "enlarge his coast" (1 Chronicles 4:10).

God has been in the process of restoring all things back to himself since the fall of Adam. Before the fall of Adam all things were in perfect order and harmony, and were submitted to God, the creator of both heaven and earth. After the fall, however, chaos filled the earth. Mankind lost its *legal* position of kingship. He was no longer connected to God spirit to Spirit. But now, through Jesus Christ, the Second Adam, we have been reborn, given the ministry of reconciliation and the ministry of restoration, the Gospel of the Kingdom. The Kingdom of God is truly at hand.

Isn't it exciting to know that you can participate with Jesus in His two ministries, redemption of sinners and the restoration of all things? You have been given the keys of the Kingdom. Now it's time to exercise that authority as a representative (image bearer) of the King of kings.

ACTION STEPS

Here are some keys that will help you discover the ministry of restoration in your life.

First, make a list of the circumstances in your life that are out of harmony with God's Word. Now find Scriptures that offer the truth that will bring change. Perhaps you are having financial challenges. If so, speak God's financial truths over your life. I like this Scripture, "My God shall provide all your need according to His riches in glory through Christ Jesus" (Philippians 4:19). As you put the Kingdom of God and His righteousness first all these things shall be added to you (Matthew 6:33).

Second, pick up a key that you can use to remind you of your authority. When you face trouble, take that key and unlock the gate that is trying to hold you back. Remember, Jesus gave the keys of the Kingdom to you and whatever you allow on earth, He allows in heaven. And whatever you forbid in your life on earth, He forbids in heaven.

In the next chapter we will discover that the New Testament Great Commission, reaching the world for Jesus, was not the first Great Commission.

APERÇU

Jesus had the ministry of the Lamb of God and the ministry of reconciliation.

The ministry of the Lamb of God deals with the redemption of sinners.

The ministry of reconciliation deals with the restoration of all things.

The born again experience, regeneration through repentance and faith in Jesus, is the prerequisite for kingship (John 3:3).

Jesus taught His apostles to announce the arrival of the Kingdom of heaven when healing the sick. (Matthew 10:7-8).

The announcement of the kingdom of heaven was not to signify a future event but a now event.

God's royal priesthood of believers are not just called to preach the Gospel of salvation. They are also called to *demonstrate the ministry of reconciliation* by using Jesus' name to overcome those things in the earth that are out of harmony with His Kingdom.

Evangelism, including "teaching them to observe all things," encompasses the salvation message (Luke 24:47) and the restoration of all things (Matthew 10:7-8).

Chapter 5

THE GENESIS MANDATE

God blessed man with the ability to govern the earth and establish the Kingdom of God. We are kingly stewards of His creation. From five blessings, what I call the Genesis Mandate, we get a tremendous understanding of God's greatness toward Adam and Eve.

Kings are fully engaged in life. The first Great Commission was the Genesis Mandate. After God created Adam and Eve He blessed them with five significant blessings. These blessings, which I call the Genesis Mandate, include the original Great Commission containing man's assignment. Scripture declares,

KINGDOM LIVING: HOW TO ACTIVATE YOUR SPIRITUAL AUTHORITY

"And God blessed them, and God said unto them, be fruitful, and multiply, and replenish the earth, and subdue it: and have dominion over the fish of the sea, and over the fowl of the air, and over every living thing that moveth upon the earth" (Genesis 1:28).

Notice that all of these blessings have to do with their ability to have dominion on the earth. Let's take a close look at these divine blessings.

FRUITFUL – *Be Productive in the Earth*

The first blessing God invoked was to be fruitful. Fruitful is the Hebrew word *parah* meaning "to grow, increase or to be productive." The word *parah* is an action verb that appears 29 times in the Old Testament. God's commandment to Adam and Eve therefore was to *be productive* in the earth.

There are two types of people in this earth, consumers and producers. Consumers are those who live their lives with little to no interest in producing anything of value. When God blessed Adam and Eve He *expected* them to become producers.

I always thought this verse had to do with bearing children. This word fruitful, however, involves far more

58   www.JonasClark.com

than bearing children and reaches into creating items that produce increase.

Be fruitful therefore means to be productive.

MULTIPLY – *Increase in the Earth*

The second blessing was to multiply. Multiply is the Hebrew word *rabah*, which occurs 226 times in the Old Testament. It means "to increase, make large, become great and grow in abundance." It should be pointed out that God's intention in this verse is repeated increase.

When one increases, they grow in number, become greater or larger. Increase, moreover, suggests steady or continual growth.

To multiply means to increase repeatedly.

REPLENISH – *Fill Everything*

The third blessing was to replenish the earth. Replenish is the Hebrew word *mala* meaning "to be filled to the fullest extent possible." Mala connotes an action that says "don't stop until there is nothing else to fill."

Replenish means, therefore, to take over everywhere.

SUBDUE – *Enslave the Earth*

The forth blessing was to subdue the earth. Subdue is the Hebrew word *kabash* meaning to enslave. God uses a strong word to describe Adam's right to demand productivity from the earth. *Kabash* also means "to *bring into subjection*, keep under, bring into bondage, make subservient and to bring under control." All of these definitions are keeping with our kingship authority to subdue the earth under Christ's rule.

God's blessing to subdue meant that the earth should become *subject to God through man.*

> God's blessing to subdue meant that the earth should become subject to God through man.

DOMINION – *Reign and Govern*

The fifth blessing was dominion. Dominion (*radah*) is the Hebrew word meaning "to reign" or "to govern." *Radah* means…

Govern

Rule

Subjugate

Tread down

Prevail

Take over

Manage

Possess.

Radah is translated "rule" 13 times in the Old Testament.

Man was blessed by the Lord to rule the earth. Adam's domain was not confined to Eden. He was blessed to govern the entire earth.

A thoughtful look around will reveal that man still possesses these Genesis blessings. In fact, man has demonstrated his ability to rule over the earth. Once I went to a show at the Miami Seaquarium in Florida, home of Lolita the killer whale. At the show was a large fish tank, the Flipper Lagoon, filled with thousands of gallons of sea water from the adjacent Biscayne Bay. Swimming around the tank were many dolphins, who were putting on quite a show as they leaped out of the water offering flips, jumps, spins and tailwalks all choreographed to jubilant Caribbean music. In the middle of the tank a petite 18-year-old girl swam to the center dressed in a vibrant red wet suit. As she approached the center of the tank she pointed her finger toward the cerulean blue Florida sky and out of the water leaped a giant killer whale. The whale's name was Lolita. She weighs over 12,000 pounds! When Lolita landed back into the tank she drenched all those sitting in the first five rows with a warm sea water shower.

The killer whale's response to a single hand motion by a young girl is a clear demonstration of man's dominion authority.

I watched a television program about fishermen who were risking their lives laboring for Alaskan King Crabs. They were filling their ships' bellies with thousands of pounds of crabs that they planned to distribute across the global market. On another program I saw thousands of acres of trees being harvested by a large lumber company to make available wood to build houses, manufacture furniture and produce paper on which to print the daily news. Yes, man is still walking in the Genesis Mandate. The difference, however, is found in man's motive.

Ruling over creation is only part of the story; we are also called to reestablish the Kingdom of our Lord and Savior. For some it is difficult to imagine themselves as rulers who have been blessed of God to take dominion. Think of governing like this... Assume for just a moment that you were sitting on a throne with a scepter of authority and whatever you said became the law of the land. Think of it; when you decree a thing it becomes law. After all, you're the king. Now think about your current spiritual condition. If you have repented of your sins and asked Jesus to come into your heart and be Lord, then you are a new creature in Christ Jesus. You are born again. Now you have the authority to decree God's will. Take a look at God's original design for your life and use your delegated authority to rule and reign with Christ Jesus – now.

KINGLY STEWARDS

God blessed man with the ability to govern the earth *and* establish the Kingdom of God. We are kingly stewards of His creation. From the five blessings, the Genesis Mandate, we get a tremendous understanding of God's greatness toward Adam and Eve, and subsequently you and me.

The five blessings were divine rights given to mankind to act as kingly representatives and governing citizens of the Kingdom of God. To review, these are the blessings contained in the first Great Commission:

+ Be Productive

+ Increase Repeatedly

- ◆ Take Over Everywhere

- ◆ Bring the Earth into Subjection

- ◆ Rule the Earth – Dominion (Kingship).

From the Genesis Mandate we discover God's expectation of us. Fruitful, multiply, replenish, subdue and dominion mean that Adam and all those born of him have the right to bring the earth into subjection. God's expectation of man is for him to govern the earth as a good steward and use it to increase and be productive repeatedly in all things – that's kingship!

It's striking to know that these five blessings never were taken away from man, even after the fall. After the fall, however, man has not been governing through an incorruptible born again spirit but through his corruptible fallen soul. Today, carnal men rule through a fallen nature that is selfish, self-willed, humanistic, carnal and dangerous. Greed causes environmental plundering and profiting from the suffering and hardship of others. We must remember that man is only a steward of this Garden of Eden we call earth. God owns it and man is called to govern it in righteousness (Deuteronomy 28:1-14).

The will of God is for His sons and daughters to bring glory to the Father by demonstrating His sovereign ownership through our delegated kingship. Scripture says,

> "Herein is my Father glorified, that you bear much fruit; so shall you be my disciples" (John 15:8).

CREATED FOR DOMINION

To sum up the five blessings in the Genesis Mandate, God has imparted to us the ability to reign and exercise dominion. Again Scripture declares,

> "And God said, Let us make man in our image, after our likeness: and let them have dominion..." (Genesis 1:26).

We gain dominion through successful conflict defined by submission to the rule of God, victory in spiritual battles, and in influence and the ability to create wealth to establish His covenant. The accumulation of spoils and dominion are the sign of victorious battle. (Matthew 12:28 speaks of binding the strong man and *spoiling* his goods. See also Luke 11:20).

You can't fail. God has created you for and with kingship authority. Lay hold of the Genesis Mandate, God's original intent for your life, and the first Great Commission, dominion.

ACTION STEPS

You were created for dominion. Productivity is vital and goals are a must. Take time right now to write out some specific goals to reach in the next 30 days, 90 days, 180 days, and one year from now. Display these goals where you can see them. Productivity is blessed and encompasses the first Great Commission.

In the next chapter we are going to find out that the world is divided into many kingdoms, all destined to become the Kingdoms of our Lord.

APERÇU

The first Great Commission was the Genesis Mandate.

After God created Adam and Eve He blessed them with five significant blessings.

The first blessing invoked was to be fruitful. Fruitful is the Hebrew word *parah* meaning "to grow, increase or to be productive."

When God blessed Adam and Eve He *expected* them to become producers.

The second blessing was to multiply. Multiply is the Hebrew word *rabah*, which occurs 226 times in the Old Testament. It means "to increase, make large, become great and grow in abundance."

The third blessing was to replenish the earth. Replenish is the Hebrew word *mala*, meaning "to be filled to the fullest extent possible."

The forth blessing was to subdue the earth. Subdue is the Hebrew word *kabash*, meaning "to enslave."

The fifth blessing was dominion. Dominion (*radah*) is the Hebrew word for "reign" or "to govern."

God blessed man with the ability to govern the earth and establish the Kingdom of God.

The five blessings were divine rights given to mankind to act as kingly representatives and governing citizens of the Kingdom of God.

The will of God is for His sons and daughters to bring glory to the Father by demonstrating His sovereign ownership through our delegated kingship.

Chapter 6

THE KINGDOM
& WORLD SYSTEMS

Every kingdom of this world that we invade with the Gospel of the Kingdom will require a spiritual fight with demonic governing authorities. Scripture offers clear instructions on overcoming the kingdoms of this world: "Submit yourselves therefore to God, resist the devil and he will flee" (James 4:7).

The world is divided into many kingdoms awaiting your arrival. Scripture declares, "The kingdoms of this world are become the kingdoms of our Lord, and of his Christ; and he shall reign for ever and ever" (Revelation 11:15).

KINGDOM LIVING: HOW TO ACTIVATE YOUR SPIRITUAL AUTHORITY

What are these kingdoms that are to become the kingdoms of our Lord anyway? Are they nations, people groups or industries? Could they include systems of commerce? This Scripture and many others describe our world as divided into many kingdoms, or domains of influence. What could these different kingdoms represent? Again, "kingdom" is the Greek word *basileia*.

A proper rendering of the word "kingdoms" is "governments" or "organized domains of rulership."

Why is it important to understand the biblical concept of kingdoms? The answer is plain, Jesus is the King of *all* kingdoms and He has given them to us. We are the image bearers of Christ. Yes, the kingdoms of this world belong to the born again believer who is charged with the responsibility to subdue all things (1 Corinthians 15:25). In fact, we are called to be good stewards of His earth; stewards who will one day be required to give an account of their stewardship.

MANY KINGDOMS, ONE CHRIST

Organized kingdoms control the lives of millions of people. For example, financial institutions control interest rates and governments set import tariffs. Defining kingdoms as domains, territories and even systems of influence that rule over people's lives may help us gain understanding. Some kingdoms may be geographical and others can be defined by realms of influence, authorities, governments, or marketplaces. Kingdoms can be seen and unseen, both natural and spiritual. The characterization of a kingdom, therefore, is a territory of rule, or a domain of power. For example, some nations are ruled by dictators or other governing bodies. There are many kingdoms of rule we can define and breakdown for identification purposes, such as:

- Nations, languages and governments

- Cultures and systems

- Business and various trades

- Finance, education and media

- Military, sports and manufacturing

- Energy, technology and science

- Arts, music and entertainment

- Medicine, religion and family

As you can see from the above list, there are many kingdoms operating in this earth. And these are just a few of them. I am sure you can think of others. The point is that all of them are destined toward the Lordship of Christ. There are many kingdoms but only one Christ. As born again followers of Christ we are called to establish God's Kingdom culture in every domain of power and influence.

DANIEL AND KINGSHIP

To understand the rulership (lordship) of Christ over kingdoms and our position as a priesthood of kings let's take a look at the Book of Daniel. The theme of the Book of Daniel is the Kingship of Christ. His teaching reveals a great conflict between earthly human rulers and spiritual rulers that culminates in the revelation that all must submit to the Most High God. Even Nebuchadnezzar, ruler of the great nation of Babylon, finally submitted to God as the "King of heaven" and acknowledged that his stately position of authority came from God (Daniel 4:34-37).

Daniel taught us that all human authority has been delegated by the Most High. In Daniel's revelation he writes,

> "And in the days of these kings shall <u>the God of heaven set up a kingdom, which shall never be destroyed;</u> and the kingdom shall not be

left to other people, but <u>it shall break in pieces and consume all these kingdoms, and it shall stand forever.</u> For just as you saw that the stone was cut out of the mountain without hands, and that it broke in pieces the iron, brass, clay, silver and gold; the great God has made this known to the king what shall come to pass in the future. The dream is certain and the interpretation is sure" (Daniel 2:4; emphasis added).

SAINTS WILL PREVAIL

This verse declares that all the kingdoms of this world shall bow to the Kingship of Christ – and His ruling kings. Jesus is the King of kings. He wants His disciples to come into their kingship. All of this points toward a Kingship movement. Scripture says,

> "The law and the prophets were <u>until John</u>: since that time the kingdom (kingship) of God is preached, and every man presseth into it" (Luke 16:16; emphasis added).

We can see that God's will is the *reestablishing of His kingship* rule in the earth through His kings. The Word declares that the saints will prevail,

"And the kingdom and dominion, and the greatness of the kingdom under the whole heaven, shall be given to the people of the saints of the most High whose kingdom is an everlasting kingdom and all dominion shall serve and obey him" (Daniel 7:27).

> Your next stop on this journey in life is rightful dominion. There is no where else to go.

Your next stop on this journey in life is rightful dominion. There is no where else to go. This establishing of Christ's Kingship rule will result in a clash of kingdoms between the kingdom of God and the dark kingdoms of this world. The good news is the saints will prevail! God has predestined the Church of Jesus Christ, which includes you, for victory.

In his book *The Day of the Saints* [2], Dr. Bill Hamon talks about a coming victorious Saints Movement. He writes,

"The victorious Saints in the Saints Movement will definitely be warriors and overcomers. Seven times the book of Revelation says that the overcomers are the only ones who will get the rewards it describes and who are privileged to rule and reign with Jesus Christ. The three

THE KINGDOM AND WORLD SYSTEMS

major things that Saints must overcome are the world, the flesh, and the devil. Those who participate in the Saints Movement will have been delivered from all worldliness, having crucified the flesh, and will be living a sanctified holy life. This puts them in position to have to fight the good fight of faith and overcome the devil."

Dr. Hamon's summary reveals the reason that spiritual warfare must be taught to every born again believer – victory. Every kingdom that we invade with the Gospel of the Kingdom will require a spiritual fight with demonic governing authorities. Scripture is clear on our mandate, "Submit yourselves therefore to God, resist the devil and he will flee." Notice he didn't say "ignore, avoid, or try to get along with." It's time for the kings of Christ to serve the eviction notice. The good news is Christ's Kingdom (rulership) is everlasting. It cannot be destroyed and will always prevail. It doesn't matter what the newspapers report or how bleak things may appear, the Kingdom of God and His kings win.

OUT OF OPPRESSIVE KINGDOMS

When we were born again we were delivered out of spiritual darkness and a paganistic system of rulership and "translated into the kingdom of His dear son" (1 Peter 2:9). We became new creatures. The realm we were delivered out from was an oppressive realm ruled by carnal men and demonic governing authorities (Ephesians 6:12). In that fallen and carnal condition we were spiritually dead in trespasses and sin and blind to the things pertaining to God and His Kingdom. As born again believers, however, we are alive unto our Lord and can see, enter, function in, advance and establish the Kingdom of God.

Not only have we been delivered out of spiritual darkness (*skotos*) but God is using every believer to continue Jesus' ministry of restoration. Scripture says,

> "Who hath delivered (rescued) us from the power (*exousia*) of darkness (*skotos*), and hath translated us into the kingdom of his dear Son: In whom we have redemption through his blood, even the forgiveness of sins: Who is the image of the invisible God, the firstborn of every creature: For by him were all things created, that are in heaven, and that are in earth, visible and invisible, whether they be thrones, or dominions (Greek *kuriotes*; dominions, powers, lordships), or principalities, (*arche*) or powers (*exousia*) all things were created by him, and for him: And he is before all things, and by him all things consist. And he is the head

of the body, the Church: who is the beginning, the firstborn from the dead; that in all things he might have the preeminence" (Colossians 1:13-18; emphasis added).

This ministry of restoration will require us to take dominion of ungodly kingdoms. Not just spiritual kingdoms but also natural kingdoms of influence. We will see the manifestation of the sons of God return the kingdoms of this world to the Kingdoms of our God. All of creation is groaning in travail waiting for the manifestation of the sons of God.

PROTECTION AND DELIVERANCE

Scripture gives us many examples of entering various lands (domains) that were governed illegally by Jehovah's enemies and God's intent to overcome every kingdom that did not submit to His Lordship such as:

"And I commanded Joshua at that time, saying, Thine eyes have seen all that the Lord your God hath done unto these two kings: so shall the Lord do unto all the kingdoms whither thou passest. Ye shall not fear them: for the Lord your God he shall fight for you" (Deuteronomy 3:21-22; emphasis added).

"And said unto the children of Israel, Thus saith
the Lord God of Israel, I brought up Israel out
of Egypt, and delivered you out of the hand
of the Egyptians, and <u>out of the hand of all
kingdoms,</u> and of them that oppressed you"
(1 Samuel 10:18; emphasis added).

You have been given both a priesthood and a kingship.
Once you begin to walk in your authority as a king
this Scripture in the Book of Revelation will be clear:

"And has made us unto our God kings and
priests: and we shall reign on the earth"
(Revelation 5:10).

KINGSHIP, A BIBLICAL PATTERN

The promise of kingship is a biblical pattern with
many examples provided from which we can learn. The
promise of kings is written in the covenant God made
with Abraham. Abraham was told that "kings" would
arise among his descendants.

"And I will make thee exceeding fruitful
(Genesis Mandate), and I will make nations
of thee, and <u>kings shall come out of thee</u>"
(Genesis 17:6; emphasis added).

Jacob said that royalty (kings) would arise from the tribe of Judah.

"The scepter (kings have scepters representing authority) shall not depart from Judah, nor a lawgiver from between his feet, until Shiloh (Christ) come; and unto him shall the gathering of the people be" (Genesis 49:10).

Jesus is the Lion of the tribe of Judah and many kings have been gathered around Him.

Solomon reigned over all kingdoms.

"And <u>Solomon reigned over all kingdoms</u> from the river unto the land of the Philistines, and unto the border of Egypt: they brought presents, and served Solomon all the days of his life" (1 Kings 4:21; emphasis added).

Solomon wasn't on vacation in his palace. Solomon reigned over "all the kingdoms" in his domain.

Jeremiah was also given authority over nations and kingdoms, even as a young man.

"See, I have this day <u>set thee over the nations and over the kingdoms,</u> to root out, and to pull down, and to destroy, and to throw down, to build, and to plant" (Jeremiah 1:10; emphasis added).

Notice that building and planting follows after rooting out, pulling down, destroying, and throwing down opposing kingdoms.

Christ has delivered you out of every oppressive kingdom. Now He wants to use you to help others get free by entering the revolution of righteousness. You have been created a new creature in Christ Jesus and given spiritual authority to represent Him. You are a king. Now you can rise as a son of God that is authorized to invade this world with the Gospel of the Kingdom, establishing Christ's Kingdom culture and thus truly occupying until He comes.

ACTION STEPS

Now that you have studied the Kingdom and world systems take a moment to define your kingdom. Ask yourself some important questions such as: Where do you work? What industry are you a part of? Where is your domain of influence? What are you a steward of? How can you start effecting change?

Jesus referred to Himself as the "Son of Man." When He did many religious leaders were shocked and wanted to kill Him. Is there some mystery we can discover in the statement? Let's find out in the next chapter.

APERÇU

A proper rendering of the word "kingdoms" is "governments" or "organized domains of rulership."

Some kingdoms may be geographical and others can be defined by realms of influence, authorities, governments, or marketplaces. Kingdoms can be seen and unseen, both natural and spiritual.

The definition of a kingdom is a "territory of rule," or a "domain of power."

Daniel taught us that all human authority has been delegated from the Most High (Daniel 2:4).

Every kingdom that we invade with the Gospel of the Kingdom will require a spiritual fight with demonic governing authorities.

The ministry of restoration will require us to take dominion of ungodly kingdoms. Not just spiritual kingdoms but also natural kingdoms of rule.

Christ has delivered you out of every oppressive kingdom. Now He wants to use you to help others get free by entering the revolution of righteousness.

Chapter 7

THE SON OF MAN

The born again believer has been endowed with a "delegated sovereignty" both natural and spiritual. As the clash of kingdoms continues we can choose to respond in a number of ways. We can surrender, withdraw, compromise, be indifferent – or become Kingdom reformers.

Kings have a grip on their purpose in life. They are willing to contribute to the greatest revolution of all time. One day Jesus performed a magnificent miracle. He healed a paralytic man. From this scene we will discover something extraordinary about the Son of Man.

"And, behold, they brought to him a man sick of the palsy, lying on a bed: and Jesus seeing their faith said unto the sick of the palsy; Son, be of good cheer; thy sins be forgiven thee. And, behold, certain of the scribes said within themselves, this man blasphemeth. And Jesus knowing their thoughts said, wherefore think you evil in your hearts? For whether is easier, to say, Thy sins be forgiven thee; or to say, Arise, and walk? But that ye may know that the Son of man hath power on earth to forgive sins, (then saith he to the sick of the palsy,) Arise, take up thy bed, and go unto thine house. And he arose, and departed to his house" (Matthew 9:2-7).

Present at this meeting were men of renown. There were the learned, the leaders, the scribes, the Pharisees, the teachers of the law, and a man in need with friends of faith. As the scene opens we see the house crowded with people eager to listen to Jesus teach. There were so many people in the house that the overflow blocked the entrance. They probably were peering in all the windows, too. The crowd of people outside included some faith-filled men determined to get help for their sick friend. Apparently this man was unable to walk. That didn't stop these men from pursuing Jesus. In fact, these emboldened men did something unimaginable. They actually climbed up on the roof with their incapacitated companion, tore off the roof tiles and lowered him into the house in the midst of Jesus' sermon. What an entrance!

Jesus was far from disturbed by the men's determination, rather He was impressed. He saw the episode as faith in action. Then Jesus said something remarkable to the disabled man,

"Son, be of good cheer, thy sins be forgiven thee" (Matthew 9:2).

This statement stunned the religious onlookers. They reasoned in their hearts that only God could forgive this man of his sins and wondered how Jesus could make such a serious proclamation. They could not accept that God was standing in their very midst. Jesus knew their hearts and responded quickly to their unspoken accusations,

"Whether is it easier to say to the sick of the palsy, thy sins be forgiven thee; or to say, arise, and take up thy bed, and walk? But that ye may know that the Son of man hath power on earth to forgive sins, (he saith to the sick of the palsy,) I say unto thee, arise, and take up thy bed, and go thy way into thine house" (Mark 2:9-11).

Jesus asked His silent accusers whether they thought it would be easier for the Son of Man to extend forgiveness or extend healing. Of course, if you are God neither act is difficult. It is part of God's nature to forgive and to heal. The point is that there is a great revelation unfolding in this verbal engagement.

Jesus referred to Himself as the *Son of Man*.

But who is the Son of Man? Those present understood exactly what Jesus meant. After all, many of them had studied the Scriptures for years. The Son of Man was the man in Daniel's vision. You see Jesus was referring to a prophetic dream that the Prophet Daniel had some thousand years prior. In this vision Daniel refers to someone called the "Son of Man." Let's take a look.

> "I saw in the night visions, and, behold, one like the Son of Man came with the clouds of heaven, and came to the Ancient of days, and they brought him near before him" (Daniel 7:13; emphasis added).

It is obvious that Jesus was referring to Himself as this person. That explains the sudden arresting offense of these religious leaders. These Pharisees knew also the rest of the Scripture, which goes on to point out that this Son of Man is the King of Glory.

> "And there was given him dominion, and glory, and a kingdom, that all people, nations, and languages, should serve him: his dominion is an everlasting dominion, which shall not pass away, and his kingdom that which shall not be destroyed" (Daniel 7:13).

From this verse we gain knowledge of seven revealing things about the Son of Man in Daniel's vision.

1. He is given dominion.

2. He is given glory.

3. He is given a kingdom (kingship).

4. All people and nations will serve Him.

5. His dominion is forever.

6. His reign is unstoppable.

7. His Kingdom can never be destroyed.

The Son of Man, therefore, is none other than Jesus the Messiah, Immanuel, the King of kings and the Lord of lords, our Mighty Deliverer. His dominion is an everlasting dominion. No wonder these religious leaders were shocked. When Jesus said He was the Son of Man, He was saying "I am the same God in Daniels' vision, the everlasting King of Glory. "

PETER'S GREAT REVELATION

Jesus used this same terminology, Son of Man, in another setting. Jesus asked His disciples this question, *"Whom do men say that I the Son of Man am?"* From this simple question Jesus revealed who He was. Let's take a look at the scene. Get ready to shout.

> "When Jesus came into the coasts of Caesarea Philippi, he asked his disciples, saying, whom do men say that I the Son of man am? And they said, some say that thou art John the Baptist: some, Elias; and others, Jeremiah, or one of the prophets. He saith unto them, But whom say ye that I am? And Simon Peter answered and said, Thou art the Christ, the Son of the living God. And Jesus answered and said unto him, Blessed art thou, Simon Barjona: for flesh and blood hath not revealed

it unto thee, but my Father which is in heaven. And I say also unto thee, that thou art Peter, and upon this rock I will build my church; and the gates of hell shall not prevail against it. And I will give unto thee the keys of the Kingdom of heaven: and whatsoever thou shalt bind on earth shall be bound in heaven: and whatsoever thou shalt loose on earth shall be loosed in heaven. Then charged he his disciples that they should tell no man that he was Jesus the Christ" (Matthew 16:13-20).

Peter stepped forward and linked the Son of Man with the Christ, "Thou art the Christ, the Son of the living God."

The Christ was the One they had been waiting for. They had heard of His coming their entire lives. He was the Messiah. He was Immanuel. He was God. He was the King of kings and the Lord of lords. His Kingdom was an everlasting kingdom that could never be destroyed and He was standing right in front of them. From these Scriptures we learn some vital lessons:

- Jesus has the power to forgive sin.

- Jesus titled Himself as the "Son of Man" a clear reference to the title given the King of Glory.

♦   Jesus is the Messiah, the Christ.

What a glorious revelation that Peter received. No wonder Peter stepped out of the boat to walk toward Jesus on the water. No wonder Peter declared, "Silver and gold have I none, but such as I have give I thee: In the name of Jesus Christ of Nazareth rise up and walk" (Acts 3:6).

THE UNSTOPPABLE REVOLUTION

Jesus both taught and preached. His message was the Gospel of the Kingdom. After John the Baptist was put in prison Jesus announced the start of His Kingship revolution.

> "Now after that John was put in prison, Jesus came into Galilee, <u>preaching the gospel of the kingdom of God,</u> and saying, the time is fulfilled, and the kingdom of God is at hand: repent ye, and believe the gospel" (Mark 1:14-15; emphasis added).

The ministry of the Son of Man, our revolutionary King is unstoppable! From what we have just studied we can surmise that the Gospel of the Kingdom contains the following truths:

1.   The earth belongs to Jesus and His kings.

2.   Jesus' Kingdom is everlasting.

3.   Jesus expects His saints to take dominion of the Kingdom.

4.   Jesus is the Son of Man and is forever the King of Glory.

5.   We are called to take the Gospel of the Kingdom into the entire world.

6.   Man's ultimate destination is not heaven but earth.

7.   The revolution has begun!

In essence every time Jesus called Himself the Son of Man He was announcing a revolution and the reestablishment of His Kingship on the earth.

KINGSHIP RESPONSE-ABILITY

Kings never surrender. When I was a young man, raised in church, many were taught to withdraw themselves from the world. The message was clear: if you enter the world there is a possibility you could become corrupted. We were taught that the world belonged to the devil, we were "just passing through," and our focus should be on holiness and the imminent return of Christ. We were to focus on the rapture that would save us from our troubles. The gathering away of the saints off the earth to enter heaven with Jesus before the great tribulation was our great escape.

It wasn't until the '80s that we began to look at our spiritual authority as believers to challenge Satan's rule. With that challenge of darkness and the subsequent victories that followed we began to recognize our ability to take control of our lives by using the Word of God as our "sword" (Ephesians 6:10-17). This was a restoration of the truth of spiritual warfare, or the authority of every born again believer to confront the powers of darkness and win.

According to Jessie Penn-Lewis, author of *"War on the Saints"* [3] in collaboration with the famous Welsh Revivalist Evan Roberts, spiritual warfare is wrestling against the powers of darkness and is part of the Christian's governing authority. She writes,

"It is only possible to wrestle against the powers of darkness, by the spirit. It is a spiritual warfare, and can only be understood by the spiritual man, that is, a man who lives by and is governed by his spirit."

Spiritual warfare is a clash with demonic rulers when a believer attempts to establish the Kingship of Christ in the spiritual realm. We have two battlefields – dominion of the earth and dominion in the spiritual realm. Dominion over demonic powers is easy.

> Spiritual warfare is a clash with demonic rulers when a believer attempts to establish the Kingship of Christ in the spiritual realm.

Scripture says, "Submit yourself to God, resist the devil and he will flee." Jesus has already disarmed all principalities and powers for us. [4]

Now 21st century believers are waking up to the fact that the world belongs to Jesus and He has given us dominion authority and a responsibility to be good stewards of this earth. It is clear that the born again believer has been endowed with a *"delegated sovereignty"* both natural and spiritual. Scripture says,

"Thou hast given him dominion over the works of thy hands; thou hast put all things under his feet" (Psalm 8:5-6).

Let's look at our Christian responsibility like this – response-ability. As the clash of kingdoms continues we have various choices of response. We can surrender, withdraw, compromise, be indifferent or become Kingdom reformers. Let's examine our choices more closely.

SURRENDER

The first option on our list of responses is to surrender. When a believer doesn't want to oppose the railing opposition to their faith in Christ they have the option to hoist the white flag of surrender, forego their rights as believers, abandon their post, and give up. Scripture says,

> "Whosoever will be a friend of the world is the enemy of God" (James 4:4).

When one surrenders to their enemy they lose all their rights, property and control over their destiny. Jesus did not call us to surrender our faith in Him and bow to our enemy.

WITHDRAW

Some believers would never go so far to surrender their faith in Christ. Instead they withdraw themselves from the battlefield of faith. They lose touch with true humanity, the plight of others, and the needs of an anguished world. This act of retreat is nothing more than self-deception and the road to spiritual defeat. Scripture declares,

> "Nay, in all these things we are more than conquerors through him that loved us" (Romans 8:37).

> "I can do all things through Christ which strengtheneth me" (Phillipians 4:13).

When a believer withdraws they remove themselves from participating in the battle for dominion and the reestablishing of Christ's Kingship. We can liken the word *withdraw* to an attitude of one who retires. Retirement is never an option in the Body of Christ or for you. To withdraw from the battle is grounds for a court marshal and jail time.

COMPROMISE

The next option for a believer is to compromise their faith. To compromise means to make concessions with the enemy. Some may think they would never do that, however, consider that one definition of the word *compromise* means to "settle for less." Anytime we

KINGDOM LIVING: HOW TO ACTIVATE YOUR SPIRITUAL AUTHORITY

attempt to shrink back from the warfare for dominion we are actually selling out. Scripture says,

> "Now the just shall live by faith: but if any man draw back, my soul shall have no pleasure in him" (Hebrews 10:38).

This Scripture is not referring to drawing back from your salvation but drawing back from the warfare that faith produces. Every believer must "fight the good fight of faith" and faith includes corresponding action. Compromise is not an option.

INDIFFERENT

Then there are believers that are indifferent to the world around them. They think if they just ignore the battles of life the warfare will go away. After all, they say, the world belongs to Satan. So they are hyper focused on escaping to heaven. This escapism attitude produces a fatalistic spirit seen in believers who intentionally avoid any active involvement in the battle for righteousness. An indifferent person attempts to remain neutral with no feelings for or against the struggles of mankind.

Another definition of *indifference* is "one who is neither cold nor hot." Jesus had some stern words for the indifferent (Revelation 3:16). As kingly believers indifference is not an option. We can never ignore what we are called to conquer.

REFORM

The final response can be to join the restoration of all things and stand among those change agents called reformers. All believers are called to run to the battle line to exercise their kingship authority and take dominion of this earth.

Scripture is replete with the stories of those with a reforming spirit. Caleb and Joshua, for example, had a "another spirit with them" (Numbers 13:30). Jesus said that we were to be "salt" and "light" to this world. As a priesthood of kings, we have "response-ability" as good stewards of this earth to establish the Gospel of the Kingdom, the rule of God, throughout the entire earth.

The Gospel of the Kingdom is the reestablishment of Christ's dominion, culture, and rule on this earth through His Body, the Church (Ephesians 3:10).

Let us be like young David who ran to the battlefield with a reforming spirit. When he heard the challenge of Goliath and saw the fear on the faces of God's warriors he boldly asked,

"Who is this uncircumcised Philistine that would challenge the armies of the living God?" (1 Samuel 17:26).

As believers we are not living in two realms on the earth. We are living "in the Kingdom" while invading the "kingdoms of this world." This world belongs to our King Jesus. There are many Scriptures that make this clear including:

- "The earth is the Lord's, and the fullness thereof; the world, and they that dwell therein" (Psalm 24:1; emphasis added).

- "If I were hungry, I would not tell thee: for the world is mine, and the fullness thereof" (Psalm 50:12; emphasis added).

- "Now therefore, if ye will obey my voice indeed, and keep my covenant, then ye shall be a peculiar treasure unto me above all people: for all the earth is mine:" (Exodus 19:5; emphasis added).

Jesus asked this question to His revolutionary recruits: "Whom do men say that I the Son of Man am?" Now He's asking you the same question. Who do you say the Son of Man is? Clearly He is the King of kings and the Lord of lords. You are a citizen of an everlasting Kingdom. You have been given some clear options in this chapter. You can join the revolution or you can compromise your faith. I am sure you have been stirred with faith to do something great with your life. Jesus said it best,

> "The time is fulfilled and the kingdom of God is at hand: repent ye, and believe the gospel" (Mark 1:15).

Christ's Kingship rule has arrived. Change the way you think, believe the Good News, and let the revolution begin!

ACTION STEPS

Jesus revealed Himself as the Son of Man who announced the greatest revolution of all time. Examine your heart to see if you have withdrawn from the battlefield or compromised your faith. If so, repent and make a decision to commit yourself to join Jesus' Kingly revolution. You have been authorized to establish the Kingdom. Start today by taking hold of your life. Determine to live in that same victorious spirit that Joshua and Caleb possessed when facing the giants of Canaan Land. This daring duo when faced with opposition declared, "Let us go up at once for we are well able." You are also well able. Take up the sword of the Spirit and the shield of faith and start establishing Christ's Kingdom culture around you.

Jesus is our pattern for kingship. He showed us how to live and taught us how to demonstrate kingship. In the next chapter we'll look more closely at how Jesus exercised His Kingship and set the pattern.

APERÇU

Jesus referred to Himself as the Son of Man.

The Son of Man was the man of Daniel's vision (Daniel 7:13).

Peter linked the Son of Man with the Christ, "Thou art the Christ, the Son of the living God" (Matthew 16:13-20).

Jesus both taught and preached. His message was the Gospel of the Kingdom (Mark 1:14-15).

Spiritual warfare is the clash with demonic rulers when a believer attempts to establish the Kingship of Christ in the spiritual realm.

We have two battlefields – dominion of the earth and dominion in the spiritual realm.

It is clear that the born again believer has been endowed with a *"delegated sovereignty"* both natural and spiritual (Psalm 8:5-6).

As the clash of kingdoms continues we have various choices of response. We can surrender, withdraw, compromise, be indifferent or become Kingdom reformers.

When one surrenders to their enemy they lose all their rights, property and control over their destiny.

Some believers would never go so far to surrender their faith in Christ instead they withdraw themselves from the battlefield of faith.

To compromise means to make concessions with the enemy.

An indifferent person attempts to remain neutral with no feelings for or against the struggles of mankind.

The Gospel of the Kingdom is the reestablishment of Christ's dominion, culture, and rule on this earth through His Body, the Church.

Chapter 8

JESUS: OUR KINGSHIP PROTOTYPE

Jesus confirmed His Kingship when He healed the sick, cast out devils, provided food supernaturally, and rebuked death, wind, storm and sea. He said repeatedly when demonstrating His Kingship, "The Kingdom of heaven has come unto you."

Jesus did more than teach His disciples, He also gave them up close and personal training day by day as He demonstrated His Kingship. One day John's disciples asked Jesus for proof of His Kingship. Jesus responded,

> "Go your way, and tell John what things you have seen and heard; how that the blind see, the lame walk, the lepers are cleansed, the deaf hear, the dead are raised, to the poor the Gospel is preached" (Luke 7:22).

His Kingship was undeniable because it was backed up with visible evidence. Hearing and seeing were part of the training process. Jesus' recruits heard Him preach the Gospel of the Kingdom and saw Him demonstrate the Gospel of the Kingdom. While preaching and demonstrating are both important, there is a distinct difference between the two.

- Preaching is *proclaiming* truth.

- Demonstrating is offering *visible evidence* of truth.

Jesus confirmed His Kingship when He healed the sick, cast out devils, provided food supernaturally, and rebuked death, wind, storm and sea. He said repeatedly when demonstrating His Kingship, "The Kingdom of heaven has come unto you." As we studied earlier, Jesus told His disciples to hold fast to that profession before sending them into the harvest fields:

> "Heal the sick that are therein and say unto them, the kingdom of God is come nigh unto you" (Luke 10:9).

What did Jesus mean in this Scripture? Could it be that whenever circumstances on the earth were changed to match circumstances in heaven that a Kingdom manifestation had come? Could it also mean that kingship is the victorious result of a clash of kingdoms, demonic darkness and sin overcome by God's magnificent light? Does the manifestation of kingship, *basileia*, mean to take dominion over darkness, sin, poverty, sickness, anti-Christ kingdoms, and even the earth itself? Since Jesus is our pattern for life, ministry, and kingship, let's find our answers in the many ways He manifested Kingship throughout His Gospel ministry.

DOMINION OVER THE UNSEEN SPIRIT REALM

Jesus didn't ignore demons nor did He teach His disciples to ignore them. The casting out of demons was proof positive of the displacement of Satan's rulership. It was

> The casting out of demons was proof positive of the displacement of Satan's rulership.

essential that Jesus bound, plundered and dismantled Satan's control. Jesus taught the "binding of the strongman" as fundamental in demonstrating kingship on earth.

Jesus didn't cast out demons because of His shed blood on Calvary. The crucifixion had not yet taken place. The atoning sacrifice of the Lamb of God had nothing to do with this demonstration of His Kingship. Jesus cast out demons because He was Immanuel. Casting out demons dealt with the ministry of the "Son of Man," the King of Glory, who was reestablishing His Kingdom on earth, assisted by the ministry of the Holy Spirit.

Everywhere Jesus went He conquered evil spirits, thus demonstrating His Lordship over them. One can only imagine the hope this bondage-breaker imparted to those who knew He was on the way to their village (Luke 8:1-2).

There is an unseen realm of demonic activity that Jesus refused to ignore. Jesus took dominion over Satan and all demonic powers. He said,

"But if I cast out devils by the Spirit of God, then the kingdom of God is come unto you.

Or else how can one enter into a strong man's house, and spoil his goods, except he first bind the strong man? And then he will spoil his house. He that is not with me is against me; and he that gathereth not with me scattereth abroad" (Matthew 12:22-30; emphasis added).

When Jesus came to this earth He did not empty Himself of His Kingship but made Himself of no reputation. When Jesus was born of a virgin and entered this world He did not leave His divinity in heaven. He was Immanuel, God in the flesh. It was His glorified state that was left behind. Scripture declares,

"Who being in the form of God thought it not robbery to be equal with God: But made himself of no reputation and took upon him the form of a servant and was made in the likeness of men: And being found in fashion as a man he humbled himself and became obedient unto death even the death of the cross. Wherefore God also hath exalted him and given him a name which is above every name: That at the name of Jesus every knee should bow, of things in heaven, and things in earth, and things under the earth; And that every tongue should confess that Jesus

Christ is Lord, to the glory of God the Father" (Philippians 2:6-11; emphasis added).

On this earth Jesus refused to let His marvelous reputation as God speak for Him. He let His works do the testifying (John 10:38). Often, people are known by their preceding reputations. Jesus, however, wanted His words, His works, and His acts to speak of Him. No preconceived ideas based on reputation were allowed. Jesus was God incarnate on earth. Jesus said "I and my Father are one" (John 10:30). When asked about the Father He said,

> "Have I been so long a time with you, and yet hast thou not known me, Philip? He that hath seen me has seen the Father" (John 14:9).

Scripture teaches us that Jesus was "equal with God" and was in fact Immanuel, God with us in the flesh. John declared,

> "And the Word was made flesh and dwelt among us, (and we beheld his glory, the glory as of the only begotten of the Father,) full of grace and truth" (John 1:14).

No, Jesus did not set aside His divinity. He made Himself of no reputation. He was and is and will forever be God Almighty!

DOMINION OVER SICKNESS AND DISEASE

Jesus demonstrated Kingship by healing the sick, the lame, diseased and infirmed. Scripture says,

> "And Jesus went about all the cities and villages, teaching in their synagogues, and preaching the gospel of the kingdom, and <u>healing every sickness and every disease among the people</u>" (Matthew 9:35; emphasis added).

Jesus opened the blind eyes of many, including two sightless men that followed Him crying out for mercy. Jesus only asked them if they believed that He was able to heal them, an obvious prompting for faith. When they affirmed their faith,

> "Then touched he their eyes, saying, according to your faith be it unto you, and their eyes were opened" (Matthew 9:27-31).

Jesus told the disciples to do the same and say, "the kingdom of God is come nigh unto you" (Luke 10:9).

Can you imagine the impact of Jesus' ministry? There He was, Immanuel, going about healing all who were sick and oppressed of the devil for God was with Him (Acts 10:38).

Even lepers were not forgotten by Jesus. Lepers were societal outcasts. Though they were rejected, even feared, Jesus did the unthinkable: He "touched them" and they were healed.

> "And it came to pass, when he was in a certain city, behold a man full of leprosy: who seeing Jesus fell on his face, and besought him, saying, Lord, if thou wilt, thou canst make me clean. And he put forth his hand, and touched him, saying, I will: be thou clean. And immediately the leprosy departed from him" (Luke 5:12-15; emphasis added).

A famous evangelist to Africa and founder of the Divine Healing Rooms in Spokane, Washington in the early 20th century, John G. Lake believed that dominion over sickness belonged to the born again Christian and was the result of the triumphant resurrection of Jesus.

> "It is the spirit of dominion when restored to the Church of Christ, that will bring again

the glory-triumph to the Church of God throughout the world, and lift her into the place, where, instead of being the obedient servant of the world, and the flesh, and the devil, she will become the divine instrument of salvation in healing the sick, in the casting out of devils (demons), and in the carrying out of the whole program of Jesus' ministry, as the early Church did." [5]

Jesus demonstrated God's love to all and no physical ailment or demon power was too great for Him. In one of His services there was a crippled man with a withered hand. The religious scribes and Pharisees were also in the service but were looking for a way to discredit Jesus because they thought it a sin to heal on the Sabbath. Scripture says,

"He saith unto the man, <u>stretch forth thine hand. And he stretched it out: and his hand was restored whole as the other</u>" (Mark 3:1-6; emphasis added).

Jesus did not compromise in the face of religious criticism. He did the will of God; He healed the man and in doing so He demonstrated His Kingship.

DOMINION OVER STORMS

Jesus' Kingship did not stop with devils and disease. Indeed, Jesus did what others had never seen before. He took dominion over nature, even commanding storms to calm down. Jesus took dominion over storms and seas by rebuking the wind and the raging waters.

> "And they came to him, and awoke him, saying, Master, master, we perish. <u>Then he arose, and rebuked the wind and the raging of the water: and they ceased, and there was calm.</u> And he said unto them, where is your faith? And they being afraid wondered, saying one to another, what manner of man is this! <u>For he commandeth even the winds and water, and they obey him</u>" (Luke 8:22-25; emphasis added).

This is a magnificent example of Jesus' Kingship. When He rebuked the wind it "ceased." This means the wind gave up its fight and quit. Not even the wind could resist His Kingship. Jesus is our hope. Even when storms blow against our lives we can depend on Him to rebuke the wind and watch it surrender in utter defeat.

DOMINION OVER DEATH

Jesus also demonstrated His Kingship by turning water into wine (John 2:1-11) and even rebuking death. Of all He did, dominion over death was the proof that He was and is God Almighty.

Lazarus was dead and buried when Jesus arrived at his tomb. His sisters, Mary and Martha, were filled with grief and tears. When Mary saw Jesus she fell at His feet and said, "Lord, if thou had been here, my brother would not have died." Jesus was disturbed at the sight. He approached the grave and commanded they roll the great stone away that sealed the entrance to Lazarus' tomb. Martha reminded Jesus that her brother had been buried four days. Jesus responded by saying,

> "If you would only believe you will see the glory of God." Then with a loud voice He cried out, "Lazarus, come forth!" Then to the amazement of all Lazarus came out of the grave, grave clothes and all. Jesus said, "Loose him and let him go" (John 11:38-42).

MARKETPLACE DOMINION

Today it's easy to forget that God is our source. Jesus reminded all that He is our true provider. One day

Jesus taught Peter, a veteran fishermen, that He was the Lord of commerce. After fishing all night and catching nothing, Jesus told Peter to try again,

> "<u>Launch out into the deep, and let down your nets for a draught.</u> And Simon answering said unto him, Master, we have toiled all the night, and have taken nothing: nevertheless at thy word I will let down the net. And when they had this done, they enclosed a great multitude of fishes: and their net broke. And they beckoned unto their partners, which were in the other ship, that they should come and help them. And they came, and filled both the ships, so that they began to sink. When Simon Peter saw it, he fell down at Jesus' knees, saying, depart from me; for I am a sinful man, O Lord. For he was astonished, and all that were with him, at the draught of the fishes which they had taken" (Luke 5:1-11; emphasis added).

Peter and his crew were experienced fishermen and hard workers. This testimony teaches us that Jesus is our source. Peter could have said, "Jesus you are a carpenter and I the fishermen. What do you know about my business?" Instead Peter pressed into the Kingdom in obedience to the word of His Lord. Peter's prosperity was waiting for him on the other side of his obedience. Jesus is Lord of the harvest.

From these Scriptures, and many not listed here, we discover that Jesus demonstrated His Kingship by taking dominion over many things, from poverty, lack and commerce to demons, sickness and storms. I can't think of a more fitting Scripture to close this chapter than,

> "Jesus Christ the same yesterday, and to day, and for ever" (Hebrews 13:8).

Now it's time to consider what Jesus said to His disciples,

> "Verily, verily, I say unto you, He that believeth on me, the works that I do shall he do also; and greater works than these shall he do; because I go unto my Father. And whatsoever ye shall ask in my name, that will I do, that the Father may be glorified in the Son. If ye shall ask any thing in my name, I will do it" (John 14:12-14).

ACTION STEPS

Jesus said that you would do greater works than His. Perhaps you have never considered the possibilities.

Start today to see yourself as a miracle worker. Determine to enter the exciting revolution of dominion. Jesus gave you authority in the unseen spirit world by using His name. If depression is attacking you, use His name. If fear is trying to hold you back, use His name. If you lack wisdom in a certain area, Scripture says,

> "If any man lacks wisdom, let him ask of God that giveth to all men liberally and upbraideth not and it shall be given him" (James 1:5).

In the next chapter we will explore the believer's mandate to demonstrate kingship. Are you ready to enter the exciting world of kingship?

APERÇU

Jesus both preached and demonstrated the Gospel of the Kingdom (Luke 7:22).

Preaching is proclaiming truth.

Demonstrating is offering visible evidence of truth.

Jesus confirmed His Kingship when He healed the sick, cast out devils, provided food supernaturally, and rebuked death, wind, storm and sea. He said repeatedly when demonstrating His Kingship, "The Kingdom of heaven has come unto you."

The casting out of demons was proof positive of a displacement of Satan's rulership.

When Jesus came to this earth He did not empty Himself of His Kingship but made Himself of no reputation (Philippians 2:6-11).

Jesus was "equal with God" and was in fact Immanuel, God with us in the flesh (John 1:14).

Jesus took dominion over death. Of everything He did this was the proof that He was and is God Almighty.

Peter pressed into the Kingdom in obedience to the word of the Lord. His prosperity was waiting for him on the other side of his obedience.

Jesus demonstrated His Kingship and took dominion over many things from poverty, lack, commerce, demons, sickness, and storms.

Chapter 9

DEVELOPING
A KINGSHIP
MENTALITY

A person who cannot change his thinking cannot change his life. Thoughts shape our lives. To enter kingship we must learn to think like kings and then we will act like kings. Kings hold the keys to authority.

Kings think different. Kingship is not just a title. Kingship requires us to act like kings. Before we can act like kings we must first develop a kingship mentality. Developing a kingship mentality will require a change of thinking. A person who cannot change his thinking cannot change his life. Thoughts shape our lives. To enter kingship we must learn to think like kings and then we will act like kings. Kings hold the keys to authority.

Jesus gave you the keys of the Kingdom. Those keys are not for just anyone, they are for those that hold to the truth that Jesus is the Christ, the Son of the Living God. Those keys of the Kingdom represent your kingship authority. Jesus told His disciples that they would do even "greater works" than He did. Scripture promises,

> "Verily, verily, I say unto you, He that believeth on me, the works that I do shall he do also; and greater works than these shall he do; because I go unto my Father" (John 14:12).

In the previous chapter we reviewed some of the demonstrations of Jesus' Kingship. In this chapter we will look at some of the things that the born again believer can do to express his or her kingship as sons and daughters of God. Let's explore the possibilities.

OUR KINGDOM RIGHTS

The question will arise, especially from the religious naysayer, "Is the believer's kingship supposed to manifest now or after one's death and resurrection?" Obviously no one completely understands all of the "mysteries of the Kingdom." I submit, however, that all born again believers have been given the keys of the Kingdom of God for use right here and right now. The keys of the Kingdom are the rights of kings to establish the Kingdom of Christ on the earth. The Kingdom of God is not just a heavenly realm. The Kingdom of God is all around you. I believe the Holy Spirit will help you see your kingship rights and authority if you ask Him. Scripture says,

> "And when he was demanded of the Pharisees, when the kingdom of God should come, he answered them and said, the kingdom of God cometh not with observation: Neither shall they say, Lo here! Or, lo there! For, behold, <u>the kingdom of God is within you</u>" (Luke 17:20-21; emphasis added).

Scripture makes it clear that the Kingdom of God is here right now – within the born again believer. Scripture also reveals that the priesthood of kings should rule and reign on the earth (Revelation 1:6, 5:10). We have already discussed that believers are partakers in Jesus' continued ministry of restoration and the establishing of His Kingdom. So how exactly does a believer demonstrate kingship? The answer is simple: by doing what Jesus said we can do – the greater works.

Kingship is not just a title. Kingship requires action. Before we can act like kings, however, we must first develop a *kingship mentality*. We must learn to think like kings. Kings are overcomers. Some might say, "I will believe it when I see it," but I am convinced that you will see it *after* you believe it.

OVERCOMING THE KINGDOMS OF THIS WORLD

God expects nothing less of His sons and daughters than to be overcomers. Scripture declares,

> "The kingdoms of this world have become the kingdoms of our Lord, and of his Christ and he shall reign forever and ever" (Revelation 11:15).

Whether "the kingdoms of this world" are sickness, poverty, false religions, secular humanism, anti-Christ spirits, corrupted strongholds in the minds of men, or unrighteous economic systems and industries believers are called to overcome them; to take dominion through victorious conquest for the glory of Christ.

The truth is that *God expects us to act like kings and rulers*. The born again believer demonstrates his kingship through conflict with unrighteousness. We are a blood bought royal priesthood called to enforce His will in our lives and carry His Gospel of the Kingdom throughout all the nations (Matthew 24:14). So we not only have the authority and power to exercise our kingship we have the responsibility to enforce Kingdom rule.

Still, some believers have a misconception concerning the Christian's regal status. They operate on the false premise that Christians are not yet kings in any sense, but will become kings only when Jesus returns for His Church. Granted, we have yet to see the fullness of Jesus' Kingship restoration, but history has provided us with a record of progressive restoration of truths that empower us to establish the Kingdom of God.

Let's take a look at some of the truths the Holy Spirit is revealing about the believer's kingship.

KINGS HAVE A DOMAIN

All kings have a domain. A domain is one's place of authority. It is the realm where you have the most influence. Scripture speaks of domains. The Greek word *metron* specifically means a territory of rule. The Apostle Paul explained this in his epistle to the church at Corinth:

"But we will not boast of things without our measure, but according to the measure (*metron*) of the rule which God hath distributed to us, a measure to reach even unto you" (2 Corinthians 10:13).

From the housewife to the postman, all of us have some measure of authority and influence. As we understand our kingship we will be able to exercise more influence and governing authority as a priesthood of kings.

If you are a son or daughter of God, then you have been authorized to govern in your domain (Ephesians 2:10).

KINGS HAVE INFLUENCE

Kings also have influence. Influence is the ability to shape, give direction and evoke change. As kings we have the power to affect the lives of thousands of people.

That ability to bring about positive change in your domain is called influence. At home or in the workplace every born again believer can do something that effects godly influence around them.

KINGS HAVE AUTHORITY

Kings have authority. Authority is the power to act. Authority is the right to enforce the Word of God, judge, determine, administrate, and command. There are three types of authority given to every born again believer.

> There are three types of authority given to every born again believer.

1. You have the right to take dominion over the earth (Genesis 1:26-27). We referred earlier to this as the Genesis Mandate, the first Great Commission.

2. You have the right to take dominion in the spirit realm. Jesus said,

"Behold I give unto you power to tread on serpents and scorpions, and over all the power of the enemy and nothing shall by any means hurt you" (Luke 10:19).

Serpents and scorpions are metaphors for demon powers operating in the unseen spirit world.

3. You have a right to enforce the Word of God in your life.

In the Gospel of Matthew, Jesus reveals keys as symbols of authority and laws of the Kingdom:

"And I will give unto thee the keys of the Kingdom of heaven: and whatsoever thou shalt bind on earth shall be bound in heaven: and whatsoever thou shalt loose on earth shall be loosed in heaven" (Matthew 16:19).

God has delegated authority, or keys, to His sons and daughters so they can rule here on the earth and assist Christ in the establishment of His Kingdom. Jesus' kings have been given the power to act on His behalf. Let's look at some additional Scriptures to drive this truth home.

"For the kingdom of God is not in word, but in power" (1 Corinthians 4:20).

"Where the word of a king is, there is power" (Ecclesiastes 8:4).

"Fear not, little flock; for it is your Father's good pleasure to give you the kingdom" (Luke 12:32).

KINGS GOVERN

Kings are called to govern. To govern means to administrate the authority that you have been given to reign as a king. Every government has guidelines that rulers follow. The government of God has a constitution. A constitution is a set of guidelines that define the rights of its membership. God's constitution is the Word of God. By the Word of God all the citizens of the Kingdom can govern themselves and their domains of influence accordingly.

To put it another way, if we expect to rule in the Kingdom of God, we must rule and be ruled by the Word of God. Jesus, our King, ruled and was ruled by the Word of God. He explained,

> "It is written man shall not live by bread alone, but by every word that proceedeth out of the mouth of God" (Matthew 4:4).

The Apostle Paul went on to explain that,

> "All Scripture is given by inspiration of God, and is profitable for doctrine, for reproof, for correction, for instruction in righteousness; That the man of God may be perfect, thoroughly furnished unto all good works" (2 Timothy 3:15-16).

We cannot govern unless we are submitted to the rules and principles established in the Word of God. The rules we are supposed to live by have already been written (Joshua 1:8). Through His Word the royal priesthood of kings can govern themselves and their territories.

KINGS JUDGE AND DECREE

Kings make decisions. When kings govern they render decisions called judgments. Those judgments lead to decrees. Our guidelines for judgment, of course, are written throughout the Word of God. Scripture says:

> "A divine sentence is in the lips of the king: his mouth transgresseth not in judgment" (Proverbs 16:10).

> "A wise king scattereth the wicked, and bringeth the wheel over them" (Proverbs 20:26).

Kings who have good judgment walk in discernment and know what is going on in their domains of influence. Scripture says,

"It is the glory of God to conceal a thing: but
the honor of kings is to search out a matter"
(Proverbs 25:2).

Not only do kings render judgments, they also
make decrees. To decree means to render a decision
and make an announcement. Scripture says,

"As it is written, I have made thee a father of
many nations, before him whom he believed,
even God, who quickeneth the dead, and
calleth those things which be not as though
they were" (Romans 4:17).

Every promise written in the Word of God belongs
to you. Abraham had the right to act like a king and
"calleth those things which be not as though they were."
What a great promise to every believer. It doesn't matter
what your life looks like today, you have the right to use
God's Word to make it line up with His will. Make a
decision today to act like a king.

KINGS ARE AMBASSADORS

Jesus' kings are ambassadors. Ambassadors are the
highest ranking government officials and representatives
of a kingdom. Scripture says,

"Now then <u>we are ambassadors for Christ,</u> as though God did beseech you by us: we pray you in Christ's stead, be ye reconciled to God" (2 Corinthians 5:20; emphasis added).

Christ's earthly representatives are His priests and kings who have been given *diplomatic authority.* The Old Testament lists various duties of ambassadors as special representatives: envoys, mediators and messengers.

ENVOY

God's ambassadors are envoys. An envoy is a special representative who acts as a government agent. The Hebrew word *tsayr* (ambassador) means "to act as an envoy," or selected delegate (Joshua 9:4; Proverbs 13:17; Isaiah 18:2; Jeremiah 49:14; Obadiah 1:1). Every believer is an envoy of Christ. You have been authorized to represent the will of God.

MEDIATOR

Ambassadors convey the policies of their government to others. They are, in effect, mediators. The Hebrew word *luwts* (ambassador) lends meaning to an ambassador's act to give voice to a government's guidelines and practices (2 Chronicles 32:31). As we lay firm to our status as kings we recognize our right to voice Christ's moral judgments and Kingdom policies to those in our domain of influence.

Don't let secular humanists stop you from conveying God's heart in society. You are an ambassador of Christ. This world needs clear direction, moral leadership, and hope for a brighter tomorrow.

MESSENGER

Ambassadors are also messengers. The Hebrew word *malak* means "to dispatch a messenger" (2 Chronicles 35:21; Isaiah 30:4; 33:7; Ezekiel 17:15). In the New Testament the Greek word *presbeuo* is used to designate those who speak the will of God (2 Corinthians 5:20; Ephesians 6:20). As kings we have been charged with a duty to speak the Word in season and out of season, when it's popular and when it's not popular. We are His messengers. What an honor it is to represent the Kingdom of God. You are His ambassador. You are a king.

It's also interesting to note that historically it was an insult to the king who sent an ambassador to harm his representative (2 Samuel 10:5). Scripture declares, "No weapon formed against you shall prosper."

KINGS ARE PROSPEROUS

Kings are prosperous. Property ownership, for example, is a fundamental function of one's kingship. David is a pattern of a warring king who fought his way through to affluence. In spite of all the warfare he went through to establish the Kingdom of God in his lifetime he was very wealthy. Scripture describes his wealth:

> "Now, behold, <u>in my trouble</u> I have prepared for the house of the Lord an hundred thousand talents of gold, and a thousand thousand talents of silver; and of brass and iron without weight; for it is in abundance: timber also and stone have I prepared; and thou mayest add thereto" (1 Chronicles 22:14; emphasis added).

Gaining finances without hard work and spiritual warfare is a fairy tale. Like David, you will have to contend for dominion. The good news is that, like David, you will win. Why is prosperity a part of the kingship message? Because kings need finances to influence and govern. As a king you can depend on Christ to help you. Our King is also our provider. When God delivered His people from Egyptian bondage He made sure they had some money.

"And I am sure that the king of Egypt will not let you go, no, not by a mighty hand. And I will stretch out my hand, and smite Egypt with all my wonders which I will do in the midst thereof: and after that he will let you go. <u>And I will give this people favor in the sight of the Egyptians: and it shall come to pass, that, when ye go, ye shall not go empty:</u> But every woman shall borrow of her neighbor, and of her that sojourneth in her house, jewels of silver, and jewels of gold, and raiment: and ye shall put them upon your sons, and upon your daughters; and ye shall spoil the Egyptians" (Exodus 3:19-22; emphasis added).

Being a steward of nothing is simply not biblical. When God delivered the children of Israel out of Egypt He delivered them with silver, gold and garments. It takes prosperity to demonstrate kingship. Jesus has already made provision for us. Scripture declares,

"For ye know the grace of our Lord Jesus Christ, that, though he was rich, yet for your sakes he became poor, that ye through his poverty might be rich" (2 Corinthians 8:9).

Some dismiss any kingship wealth building strategy because they see prosperity as anti-spiritual. Jesus addressed this by explaining,

> "There is no man that hath left house, or brethren, or sisters, or father, or mother, or wife, or children, or lands, for my sake, and the gospel's, <u>But he shall receive an hundredfold now in this time, houses, and brethren, and sisters, and mothers, and children, and lands, with persecutions; and in the world to come eternal life.</u> But many that are first shall be last; and the last first" (Mark 10:29-31; emphasis added).

Notice He uses the term "now in this time" with warfare. Kingship wealth building is vital in establishing the Kingdom of God on earth. Prosperity belongs to you. To obtain it requires trusting Jesus as your source, but it also requires plenty of hard work, prophetic strategies, submission to His word, and a subduing spirit.

KINGS ARE WARRIORS

Kings are brave warriors for Christ. Scripture teaches that the kings of Christ enter kingship through much trouble. The Apostle Paul did a great deal to launch the Church of Jesus Christ. He made sure the people understood the warfare involved in victorious living. He confirmed the souls of the disciples,

> "...exhorting them to continue in the faith, and that we must through much tribulation enter into the kingdom of God" (Acts 14:22; emphasis added).

So we learn that kings not only rule but also fight. The American revolutionary Patrick Henry said,

> "The battle, sir, is not to the strong alone; it is to the vigilant, the active, the brave."

Today the Holy Spirit is calling Christ's army of kings into action.

Growing up in church I was taught that all the warfare was over when Jesus, dying on the cross, said "It is finished" (John 19:30). However, that left me with questions. If all things were finished, then why were there still sick people in the world? Why were there children going to bed hungry? Why were there almost 1 billion people in this world living in poverty? And why was I having so much trouble? Could it be possible when Jesus said "It is finished" that He was referring to His work as the Lamb of God in offering His atoning blood as a sacrifice for sin and not the restoration of all things? Could it be possible that you and I as a royal priesthood of kings still have a work to do? Could it be possible that all the enemies of Jesus have not yet been subdued? Is there still warfare to complete? Let's take a look at this Scripture for some insight.

"But now is Christ risen from the dead, and become the first fruits of them that slept. For since by man came death, by man came also the resurrection of the dead. For as in Adam all die, even so in Christ shall all be made alive. But every man in his own order: Christ the first fruits; afterward they that are Christ's at his coming. Then cometh the end, when he shall have delivered up the kingdom to God, even the Father; when he shall have put down all rule and all authority and power. For he must reign, till he hath put all enemies under his feet. The last enemy that shall be destroyed is death. For he hath put all things under his feet. But when he saith all things are put under him, it is manifest that he is accepted, which did put all things under him. And when all things shall be subdued unto him, then shall the Son also himself be subject unto him that put all things under him, that God may be all in all" (1 Corinthians 15:20-28; emphasis added).

This Scripture makes it clear: you and I are in a battle for dominion. The war's not over. We know that all enemies are yet to be put under His feet because people are dying every day.

Being a king means being at war with the powers of darkness. No longer are we coming to church only to be blessed. We *are* getting blessed but we are also being trained as kings who understand the mandate of spiritual warfare to "put all enemies under His feet." Establishing Christ's Kingdom requires confronting and subduing the kingdoms of darkness. The pattern for possessing (Hebrew *yarash*) the Promised Land is found throughout Scripture. To *possess* means to occupy by displacing the former occupants. (See Joshua 1:1-11; 6:2; 23:5-12.)

KINGS USE THE NAME OF JESUS

Understanding your right to use the name of Jesus is vital in developing a kingship mentality. Jesus has given His kings the right to use His name. Scripture declares,

> "That at the name of Jesus every knee should bow, of things in heaven, and things in earth, and things under the earth; And that every

tongue should confess that Jesus Christ is Lord, to the glory of God the Father" (Philippians 2:10-11; emphasis added).

When you use the name of Jesus you are speaking on His behalf and with His authority. The Word teaches us the pattern for using the name above all names. Jesus did not stop with the name only. Jesus gave His disciples authority to use His name coupled with the power to heal the sick, cleanse the lepers, raise the dead, and cast out devils.

"And as ye go, preach, saying, the kingdom of heaven is at hand. Heal the sick, cleanse the lepers, raise the dead, cast out devils: freely ye have received, freely give" (Matthew 10:7-8).

His name and His Kingdom are connected. Jesus said believers would demonstrate kingship saying,

"These signs shall follow them that believe: In my name they shall cast out devils: they shall speak with new tongues; They shall take up serpents; and if they drink any deadly thing, it shall not hurt them; they shall lay hands on the sick, and they shall recover" (Mark 16:17-18; emphasis added).

We know this is true. The evangelist Philip preached the Gospel of the Kingdom and demonstrated kingship through many signs and wonders (Acts 8:1-12). The Apostle Paul preached kingship, "disputing and persuading things pertaining to the kingdom of God" (Acts 19:8). Throughout the ages, believers have been preaching, teaching and demonstrating the Kingdom of God with signs and wonders following.

You, too, have a right to continue the restoration works of King Jesus. Use His name. It belongs to you. Remember, His promise to you is,

> "He that believeth on me, the works that I do shall he do also; and greater works than these shall he do; because I go unto my Father" (John 14:12).

You are a king within a kingdom. Now take your authority and use His name to advance His Kingdom.

ACTION STEPS

You can develop a kingship mentality. Begin by seeing yourself as a king; one who possesses certain delegated rights and privileges. You have, for example, the right to act like your Father in heaven. You have the right to act like God's friend Abraham, who called those things that be not as though they were.

Take a look at where you live and work. That is your realm of influence. Now begin to exercise your authority to represent Jesus in your domain. Your presence, input, knowledge, and morals all offer kingship influence.

Throughout this book you have been learning about your royal priesthood and authority to establish the Kingdom of God. In the next chapter we are going to examine some strategies for manifesting the Kingdom of God in your life.

APERÇU

Jesus told His disciples that they would do even "greater works" than He did (John 14:12).

All born again believers have been given the Kingdom of God right here and right now (Luke 17:20-21).

Before we can act like kings it is vital to develop a kingship mentality.

Kingship is demonstrated authority that comes about after a victorious spiritual warfare with the kingdoms of darkness.

A domain is one's place of authority. It is the realm where you have the most influence.

As we understand our kingship we will be able to exercise more influence and governing authority as a priesthood of kings.

Influence is the ability to shape, give direction and evoke change.

Authority is the power to act.

God has delegated authority to His spiritual sons and daughters to rule here on the earth and to assist Christ in the establishment of His Kingdom.

If we expect to rule in the Kingdom of God, we must rule and be ruled by the Word of God.

To govern means to administrate the authority that you have been given to reign as a king.

Ambassadors are the highest ranking government officials and representatives of another kingdom.

An envoy is a special representative who acts as a government agent.

Being a steward of nothing is simply not biblical (Exodus 3:19-22).

Scripture teaches that the kings of God enter kingship through much trouble (Acts 14:22).

When you use the name of Jesus you are speaking on His behalf and with His authority (Philippians 2:10-11).

Chapter 10

KINGSHIP STRATEGIES & TACTICS

A revolutionist insists on a different way of thinking and living – a change. Jesus' revolution is one of righteousness. It confronts opposing forces wherever they appear. His revolution is found in the establishing of the Kingdom of God on the earth and He wants to use you as a 21st century revolutionary.

History books are full of great strategists, like the French General Napoleon Bonaparte, who was a military mastermind, and Julius Caesar, who balanced military and political strategy with supple genius. A strategy is a plan of action that targets a desired result. Of course, Jesus is the greatest strategist of them all – and He is our prototype King.

So as you learn about kingship, it will require you to make some changes in the way you live. The information you have learned in this book should be helping to change your perspective of life and ministry. Now you have to download that information into your life and apply it on a daily basis. That requires a strategy. We have already discussed several strategies for activating your kingship.

Now let's examine some other tactics you can execute, such as joining the kingship revolution, resisting the modern-day Canaanites and activating Kingdom economics.

THE KINGSHIP REVOLUTION

The first strategy for manifesting the Kingdom is to join the revolution. Hopefully by now you have made a decision to enlist.

John the Baptist prophesied the coming revolution (Matthew 3:11) and Jesus announced the revolution's arrival when He said,

"The time is fulfilled, and the kingdom of God
is at hand: repent ye, and believe the Gospel"
(Mark 1:15).

When Jesus commanded repentance, He wasn't just
suggesting that men seek forgiveness of their sin. He
was charging all within the sound of His voice to change
their thinking. See, a revolutionist insists on a better
way of thinking and living, a change. Jesus' revolution is
a righteous revolution. It confronts all opposing forces
whenever and wherever they rear their ugly heads. His
revolution intends to establish the Kingdom of God on
the earth and He wants to use you to do it.

When David ran to the battlefield he heard Goliath
taunting the army of God. When his brethren, filled
with fear, challenged David's purpose for coming, he
asked them this question: "Is there not a cause?" (1
Samuel 17:29). David proved his metal by asking
another question: "Who is this uncircumcised Philistine
that he would challenge the armies of the living God?"
We, too, have a just cause to accomplish. Our cause is
the advancement of Christ's purposes. Scripture tells
us we are God's workmanship, created for good works.
We are the salt of the earth, the light of the world, and
a city set on a hill (Matthew 5:13-14).

The greatest fulfillment a man can ever experience
is spending his years in the perfect will of God. Jesus
instructs believers to model a kingship lifestyle,

"Let your light so shine before men, that they may see your good works, and glorify your Father which is in heaven" (Matthew 5:16).

What greater cause can there be than establishing the Kingdom of God in our lives, families, country and nations of the world? (Acts 1:8) Jesus made clear that there would be a warfare against the establishing of His Kingdom when He told people to,

"Think not that I am come to send peace on earth: I came not to send peace, but a sword" (Matthew 10:34).

But Jesus also promised us the victory in battle. Just as David defeated Goliath, we, too, as kingly revolutionaries, will defeat our spiritual enemies with one smooth stone. Yes, there is a cause and you have been born for such a time as this. What a great time to be alive!

RESIST THE CANAANITES

The most common battle for born again believers is the battle for financial breakthrough.

Our next strategy for entering into kingship is to defeat the Canaanites. When God delivered His people out of Egyptian bondage He gave them the promise of another land. This land was known as the Promised Land. It was a land occupied by various adversaries called Canaanites, Hittites, Amorites, Perizzites, Hivites, and Jebusites (Exodus 3:8). These were *fierce* enemies all. God's commandment to His covenant people was to "possess" the land (Joshua 1:11). To possess *(yaresh)* meant to occupy by driving out the former occupants.

The most commercial tribe in the Promised Land was the Canaanites. These were the merchants. Today we can liken Canaanites to those who offer "merchant cards" commonly referred to as credit cards.

In fact, merchant cards are nothing more than snares to everyone but the most disciplined consumers. They offer quick and easy access to capital – but they do so at a dear price. Credit card companies are charging upwards of 20 percent interest, plus various other additional fees. At that rate of interest they double their money every 3.6 years (based on the law of 72)[6]. That means if you pay only the minimum payment, your debt doubles every 3.6 years. Currently, nearly half of all U.S. households carry a balance. In 2005, these households averaged $9,312 in credit card debt at 13.3 percent interest, more than double the level of a decade ago.[7] Overall, banks are collecting record penalty fees from credit cards. This year, U. S. banks are expected to receive over *$16.5 billion*, up 11 percent from last year, from late, over-the-limit and other penalty fees, according to R. K. Hammer, a bank consulting firm. Did you notice that the American government changed the bankruptcy laws in 2005 to further protect the credit card companies?

These Canaanites are crafty and scientific in their approach to put you in financial bondage with "universal default penalties" in which cardholders' interest rates are raised up to 30 percent if you pay late with any other creditors. Other snares include ATM machines in the grocery stores and shopping centers for that quick cash advance with a four-dollar transaction fee, interest only real estate loans that leave you paying a much higher mortgage in the long-run, and many other cunning methods to get you in debt. Scripture is clear,

"The rich ruleth over the poor, and the borrower is servant to the lender" (Proverbs 22:7).

Credit cards should never be used to finance things that you cannot afford. They should only be used for emergencies and convenience. Being in bondage to the Canaanite merchants is paramount to violating the mandate to "possess" the land. We are to be the head and not the tail, above and not beneath (Deuteronomy 28:13).

The Canaanite kingdom is not limited to credit cards; its focus is universal financial dominance. Now is the time to look at the Canaanites from a kingship perspective. You can't conquer those to whom you have become slaves. You can't serve two masters, God and mammon (Matthew 6:24).

Make every effort right now to get free from consumer debt! Easy money is the deceptive weapon of the 21st century Canaanites. Just as Israel of old was called to conquer the Canaanites, so are you. God wouldn't tell you to dispossess them if it couldn't be done. He will give you the wisdom and grace to overcome them.

Take courage, you can do it! The novelist Ernest Hemmingway once said that courage was grace under pressure. Scripture says that you can do all things through Christ that strengthens you. Grab hold of this promise:

> "Seek ye first the kingdom (rule) of God and His righteousness and all these things shall be added unto you" (Matthew 6:33).

ACTIVATE KINGDOM ECONOMICS

God has a Kingdom financial plan that is vital to your success as a kingship believer.

Consider the time when the nation of Israel was complaining about the benefits of serving God. They murmured,

> "It is vain to serve God: and what profit is it that we have kept his ordinance, and that we have walked mournfully before the Lord of hosts?" (Malachi 4:14)

Some have this same complaint today. They wonder if there are any financial benefits in obeying God's Word. God addressed this challenge directly by commanding His people to return unto Him with tithes and offerings.

Perhaps tithes and offerings was not the strategy you wanted to read about in activating your kingship, but the truth is that you cannot escape His road to financial success (Malachi 4:8). Don't allow yourself to shutdown now! This is critical to your understanding of unlocking your believer's kingship. Scripture declares,

> "Bring ye all the tithes into the storehouse that there may be meat in mine house, and prove me now (put me on trial) herewith, saith the Lord of hosts, if I will not open you the windows of heaven, and pour you out a blessing, that there shall not be room enough to receive it" (Malachi 4:10).

Notice the words open, windows, blessing and abundance. What a promise!

The questions still arise today, "Why should any born again believer pay tithes and give offerings?" And, "Is there any benefit in doing so?"

Paying tithes and giving offerings is central to activating the Kingdom of God for every believer. Paying tithes and giving offerings is fundamental and testifies of the Lordship of Christ. Let's take a moment to review some important truths.

1. Paying tithes and giving offerings are fundamental to Kingdom economics.

God uses the mandate of tithing to finance His purposes. Certainly God does not need our money, yet He unquestionably demands our acknowledgment of His Sovereignty over the born again believer. Adam's sin was refusing to submit to the Lordship of God. He didn't just want to be like God, he wanted to be his own god. Adam sought to be self-governing. His fall created the first humanist, man-ruled, submissive-to-no-one, rebellious person. His crime of rebellion was so serious it was punishable by death.

2. When we tithe and give offerings we acknowledge our dependence on Christ as our source.

Refusing to tithe only testifies of one's rejection of the Lordship (rulership) of Christ. Failure to pay is nothing more than robbing from God. It's theft. Even Satan knows the tithe belongs to God. He also knows that when the tithe is not paid he has every right to it. This entire book has been about God using you to establish the Kingdom of God on this earth – and that requires submitting to His Lordship, even over your finances. When submitting to His Word on tithes and offerings you leave the Canaanites economic system and enter the realm of Kingdom economics.

3. Not tithing propels us outside the benefits of kingship blessings on this earth.

Participation in the kingship of every believer requires submission to the Word of God. Failure to submit launches us back into the wilderness, symbolic of the curse (Malachi 4:9, Deuteronomy 8:15). There is no denying it, Jesus owns you. He bought you with His blood at Calvary. You can't be a lord (ruler) without submitting to "the" Lord.

4. When you pay tithes and give offerings you acknowledge God as your source for all things and the blessings of righteous dominion found in the Genesis Mandate.

GOD IS YOUR SOURCE

Your spouse, employer, business, church, or ministry is not your source. They are only a means that God uses to get finances to you. Scripture declares "But thou shalt remember the Lord thy God: for it is he that giveth thee power to get wealth, that he may establish his covenant which he swore unto thy fathers, as it is this day" (Deuteronomy 8:18). God wants to finance the Genesis Mandate: be fruitful, multiply, increase, subdue and have dominion.

5. When paying tithes and giving offerings you can expect God to rebuke the devourer.

A devourer is one who steals the fruits of your labor. The advantages of tithing are tremendous. God says,

"And I will rebuke the devourer for your sakes, and he shall not destroy the fruits of your ground; neither shall your vine cast her fruit before the time in the field, saith the Lord of hosts. And all nations shall call you blessed for you shall be a delightful land, saith the Lord of hosts" (Malachi 3:11-12).

God wants to prosper you. As you tithe and give offerings you can expect many blessings for obedience to Kingdom economics. Scripture declares,

"The Lord shall open unto you his good treasure, the heaven to give the rain unto your land in his season, and to bless all the work of thine hand and thou shalt lend unto many nations and thou shalt not borrow" (Deuteronomy 28:12).

Determine today to be faithful steward.

> It seems the poorest kings on earth are sitting in churches on Sunday morning.

In the last chapter we learned that kings have treasures, kings are prosperous and kings go to war. I've never read about a poor king in the history books. It seems the poorest kings on earth are sitting in churches on Sunday morning. Obviously pauperism is not a regal trait. If you have been faithful to tithe and give and you are still struggling financially, it could be that the power of the Canaanite merchants have enslaved you. If the Canaanites have held you captive, take courage. Your destination is victory. By activating the Kingdom economic system through paying tithes and giving offerings God, along with some financial common sense, will lead you out of bondage into freedom. Start your journey today by acknowledging Jesus as your source, avoid debt and get a handle on your finances. Determine today that you will pay tithes and give offerings to the Lord. Join the revolution, fight the Canaanites, and activate God's economic system in your life.

ACTION STEPS

God wants to give you strategies for kingship. I think one of the most effective steps you can take is to acknowledge Jesus as your source. By paying tithes and giving offerings to God you acknowledge His covenant – and that unlocks God's Kingdom economics in your life.

Next make a decision to get out of debt. Get those credit cards paid off. Every time you use that credit card for something make sure to pay it off completely at the end of the month. Don't let the Canaanites enslave you! I know lots of people that used to be in bondage to financial debt. When they renewed their mind to kingship principles and set specific goals, they got free. Now they are manifesting the promise that they are the head and not the tail, above and not beneath. Now they have finances and the freedom to advance the Gospel. You, too, can do all things through Christ Who strengthens you.

God has called you to be a world changer and a history maker. You are a king with the authority to represent Christ and establish His Kingdom on this planet. In the next chapter, you will discover the damaging effects of the escapist mentality and learn the secrets of a proactive faith.

APERÇU

A strategy is a plan of action that targets a desired result.

The first strategy for kingship is to join the revolution.

The greatest fulfillment a man can ever experience is spending his years in the perfect will of God (Matthew 5:16).

One strategy for kinship is to defeat the Canaanites (Exodus 3:8).

Canaanites are crafty and scientific in their approach to put you in financial bondage with "universal default penalties" in which cardholders' interest rates are raised up to 30 percent if they pay late with any other creditors. Other snares include ATM machines in the grocery stores and shopping centers for that quick cash advance with a four-dollar transaction fee, interest only real estate loans that leave you paying a much higher mortgage in the long-run, and many other cunning methods to get you into debt.

Easy money is the deceptive weapon of the 21st century Canaanites.

Paying tithes and giving offerings is central to activating the Kingdom of God for every believer.

Paying tithes and giving offerings is fundamental and testifies of the Lordship of Christ (Malachi 4:10).

When we tithe and give offerings we acknowledge our dependence on Christ as our source.

When you pay tithes and give offerings you can expect God to rebuke the devourer.

Chapter 11

WORLD CHANGERS & HISTORY MAKERS

The Gospel of the Kingdom is the only true gospel. It boldly proclaims that the Kingdom of God has come to the earth. It offers the Good News that, through repentance of sin, we can be restored to our kingship as believers and launched into this world with a dominion agenda. We were not created for heaven but for earth.

Kings are world changers and history makers. This book is about making people think. There is always hope for positive change when we can see the same things in a different light. Knowing that ones eschatology charts the course of life cautions us to be sure we aren't looking at old road maps in dimmed lights.

Eschatology is the study of the end of the world, the destiny of humanity, and particularly the rapture of the Church and the Second Coming of Christ. So should we be rapture-minded or dominion-minded? That question could lead you to delve into years of eschatology. Or you could just believe what Jesus told His disciples and put an end to the debate in your own soul. Jesus said that this Gospel of the Kingdom shall be preached in all the world as a witness and then the end shall come (Matthew 24:14). Has the Gospel of the Kingdom been preached in the entire world? Have we made disciples of all nations? Should we dare to consider that it is possible that Jesus is not going to return in our lifetime? And even if He did return, what is our ultimate destination anyway? Is the cross our sole focus and responsibility?

Dr. Myles Monroe in his book *"Rediscovering the Kingdom"* addresses some of these issues:

> There is no biblical evidence, however, that Jesus ever made the "born again" message the focus of His message to the crowds who thronged Him everywhere He went. The heart of Jesus' message was not about being born again; He preached about the Kingdom of God. He rarely spoke about the cross or so

many other issues that have filled the place in our sermons. He did teach on these things with His own followers and others who came seeking more knowledge. His message was quite different when dealing with the scribes and Pharisees who challenged Him. But with the common people, Jesus preached the Kingdom of God. [8]

I remember a controversy arose over what was referred to as "Kingdom Now Theology" of the late 1980s. Simply stated, the stir was over whether or not Jesus could return or rapture His Church if His kingship was not yet established in the earth by His Church. There was such a ruckus over this issue of the circumstances surrounding Jesus' coming that any truths that might have been learned were quickly replaced with a strong emphasis on getting ready for the eminent return of Christ and the rapture of the saints. In the ensuing years the best-selling Christian books and videos, over 60 million units in fact, dealt with believers being raptured and others, who were not ready, being left behind.[9] At the time I could only find a few books that promoted the authority of every believer to establish the Kingdom of God. It seems the Church was – and in many ways still is – rapture-minded.

One can only wonder if the proliferation of the rapture teaching hindered the plan of God by preparing a people to leave the earth rather than taking dominion of the earth. Yes, it's possible that the teachings led thousands to the saving grace of the Lord Jesus, too. One can only speculate. Yet when you look at the condition of our nation, the world, and the weakness of the Church to address real issues it sure appears as if we are focused too much on a rapture while ignoring our responsibility to be an image bearer of Christ. One only needs to ask if the world is becoming a better place. Is the Church speaking out? Are we trying to make things better? Or are we just looking for a way to escape?

Perhaps you have a deceased loved one who thought the Lord would return in their lifetime. I did. I had many conversations with my mother about the coming of the Lord before she passed away. But Jesus didn't come back in her lifetime. He may not come back in my lifetime or yours, either. So the question remains, what should we be doing? Do we have a responsibility to take our faith and kingship authority into the world to help make it a better place? Are we to sit idly by and watch our children and grandchildren ravished by ungodly secular humanist and anti-Christ spirits without a fight? God forbid.

> **We need to make our lives count for something.**

I think we should live like Jesus is coming today, but impact our generation with Gospel truth as if He's not going to return for many years. Yes, I believe that Jesus is coming, we need to be ready, and we need to do all we can to advance and establish the Kingship of Christ in the earth through the Gospel of Jesus Christ. We need to make our lives count for something.

AVOIDING THE ESCAPIST MENTALITY

Many know people who are "rapture-focused." Some are easy to recognize because they are tired, beat up, behind in their bills, struggle with their boss, hate their job, suffer family difficulties, endure harassment from credit card companies, or they are just plain sick of life and this world. Without a kingship focus, the daily challenges of life can produce an "escapist mentality" that is not Scriptural. This book has been about offering you hope for a brighter tomorrow. You *can* change the world around you. Your children's future is important. It's not a waste of time. You are special and God has made you unique and significant. He needs you.

As we learn to walk out our kingship Jesus will give us the victory over every unpleasant circumstance. Yes, we should look for His coming, but we must be a people that are intent on reaching the harvest fields of this world and rise into our dominion/kingship authority. The devil doesn't own this world, Jesus does. Make him bow to the name of Jesus!

My concern is that an unbalanced concentration solely on a rapture eschatology can produce a survival, escapist's mentality that drains the fight out of people. An escapist's mentality is not Scriptural. The Bible contains many verses of victorious Kingdom living:

> "Nay, in all these things we are <u>more than conquerors</u> through him that loved us" (Romans 8:37; emphasis added).

There is no conquering to do in heaven.

> "And he called his ten servants, and delivered them ten pounds, and said unto them, <u>Occupy till I come</u>" (Luke 19:13; emphasis added).

You don't need talents in heaven.

> "<u>To him that overcometh</u> will I grant to sit with me in my throne, even as I also overcame, and am set down with my Father in his throne" (Revelation 3:21; emphasis added).

There is nothing to overcome in heaven.

"Herein is my Father glorified, that ye <u>bear much fruit;</u> so shall ye be my disciples." (John 15:8; emphasis added).

God wants us to bear fruit right now.

"But the meek *shall* <u>inherit the earth;</u> and shall delight themselves in the abundance of peace" (Psalm 37:11; emphasis added).

Notice that our inheritance is earth and not heaven.

"For the promise, that he should be the <u>heir of the world,</u> was not to Abraham, or to his seed, through the law, but through the righteousness of faith" (Romans 4:13; emphasis added).

Faith is active and gives us the world as our inheritance.

"<u>Ye are the salt of the earth:</u> but if the salt has lost his savor, wherewith shall it be salted? It is thenceforth good for nothing, but to be cast out, and to be trodden under foot of men. <u>Ye are the light of the world.</u> A city that is set on a hill cannot be hid" (Matthew 5:13-14; emphasis added).

Those who are salt and light are not hiding from the world. They are proactive in their faith in Christ and active establishing His will.

"And Caleb stilled the people before Moses, and said, Let us go up at once, and <u>possess it; for we are well able to overcome</u>" (Numbers 13:30; emphasis added).

Caleb had that kingship fight in him. Like a true king he was ready to occupy.

"And they <u>overcame</u> him by the blood of the Lamb, and by the word of their testimony; and they loved not their lives unto the death" (Revelation 12:11; emphasis added).

This verse makes it clear that sin is not the only thing the born again believer must overcome. There is no sin in heaven and no him (Satan) to overcome.

Ask yourself this question: "Does the world belong to God or Satan?" If we get raptured tonight aren't we destined to come right back? Jesus told us to occupy until He returns. Interestingly, another definition of the word "occupy" means "to seize through militant conquest." This requires a different spirit in the heart of God's people.

MAINTAIN A PROACTIVE FAITH

Did the rapture eschatology produce a fatalistic, doom and gloom world view? Did it emphasize leaving the world rather than changing the world? Think about it. The restoration of all things through our kingship restoration is not a new teaching. It goes all the way back in history to Abraham, the father of faith and the friend of God. It was revealed to Abraham to bless all nations and peoples of the earth (Genesis 12:3). Abraham was told that "kings" would arise among his descendants,

> "And I will make thee exceeding fruitful, and
> I will make nations of thee, and kings shall
> come out of thee" (Genesis 17:6).

Abram didn't withdraw himself from the world. He made a significant impact. Just look at the many possessions that Abraham accumulated as he obeyed God. Those possessions empowered him with influence and those possessions accumulated because he put the Kingdom of God and His righteousness first (Matthew 6:33). God added these things to Abraham, and gave him credibility and a powerful testimony of the Most High working in his life to a pagan world.

When Abraham paid tithes to Melchizedek he was acknowledging God's kingship rule over His life. His tithing unlocked God's Kingdom economy. God responded to Abraham's tithe,

> "And he *blessed him,* and said, Blessed be Abram of the most high God, <u>possessor of heaven and earth</u>" (Genesis 14:19; emphasis added).

Abraham demonstrated his kingship to those around him. Abraham, God's man of faith was *proactive* in his faith and so should we be, too. A proactive faith demonstrates the first Great Commission, the Genesis Mandate that we studied in Chapter Five.

- Be Productive

- Increase Repeatedly

- Takeover Everywhere

- Bring the Earth into Subjection

- Rule the Earth – Kingship.

THE INCREASING GOVERNMENT

Scripture says,

> "For unto us a child is born, unto us a son is given: and the government shall be upon his shoulder: and his name shall be called Wonderful, Counselor, The Mighty God, The Everlasting Father, and The Prince of Peace. Of the increase of his government and peace there shall be no end, upon the throne of David, and upon his kingdom, to order it, and to establish it with judgment and with justice from henceforth even for ever. The zeal of the Lord of Hosts will perform this" (Isaiah 9:6-7).

Notice from this Scripture that the government of our Lord is located "upon His shoulders." This is a description of the Body of Christ, the royal priesthood.

There can never be an "increase of His government" without the increase of governing authority, dominion activity, and demonstrated kingship through Christ's priests and kings. Yes, one day the end will come as Scripture confirms,

> "Then cometh the end, when he shall have delivered up the kingdom to God, even the

Father; when he shall have put down all rule and all authority and power. For he must reign till he hath put all enemies under his feet" (1 Corinthians 15:24-25).

Until that day comes you have the grand opportunity to exercise your authority as a believer to enter your kingship.

+ Jesus reigns through His priests and kings!

Finally the Bible reveals,

"And *when* all things shall be <u>subdued</u> unto him, *then* shall the Son also himself be subject unto him (the Father) that put all things under him, that God (the Holy Spirit) may be all in all" (1 Corinthians 15:28; emphasis added).

It's obvious that all His enemies are not yet under His feet and there is still much more to accomplish.

Jesus commanded us to preach and demonstrate the Gospel of the Kingdom. He announced its arrival and gave us a way to participate in it. Jesus, the last Adam, showed us how to gain back through obedience what the first Adam lost through rebellion.

The Gospel of the Kingdom is a dominion gospel. We should never lead people to salvation and focus them solely on heaven. The apostles of old didn't preach heaven as our sole fouus and neither should we (Revelation 5:10). The Gospel of the Kingdom with Christ as its founder is the only true gospel. It boldly proclaims that the Kingdom of God has come to the earth. It promises that through repentance of sin and faith in Christ we can be restored to our kingship role as believers. It prepares us to be launched into this world with a dominion mandate. We were not created for heaven but for earth. Scripture declares of our domain,

"The highest heavens belong to the Lord, but the earth he has given to man" (Psalm 115:16).

God has called you to be a world changer and a history maker. Respond to the call. Rise up as one of His kings, take your position and "show forth the praises of him that has called you out of darkness" (1 Peter 2:9).

ACTION STEPS

You are a world changer and history maker. Avoid the escapist mentality at all cost. The newspaper does not dictate your future. A friend of mine used to have this saying, "That's just the way things are." What he meant was he had little control over his life. A kingship response to that statement is, "Yes, that's the way things are until we change them."

Jesus has no problem getting His sons and daughters to heaven. What He is trying to do is get heaven to earth. Keep your life and faith proactive. Stay productive, increase repeatedly, and rule.

Kingship is not a future event but is now. You are called to rule and reign with Christ. What good is rulership without a realm? In the next chapter you are going to discover that total conquest belongs to you.

APERÇU

Eschatology is the study of the end of the world, the destiny of humanity, and particularly the rapture of the Church and the Second Coming of Christ.

We should live like Jesus is coming today, but impact our generation with Gospel truth as if He's not going to return for many years.

Many know people who are "rapture-focused." Some are easy to recognize because they are tired, beat up, behind in their bills, struggle with their boss, hate their job, suffer family difficulties, endure harassment from credit card companies, or they are just plain sick of life and this world.

An unbalanced concentration solely on a rapture eschatology produces a survival, escapist mentality that drains the fight out of people.

Did the rapture eschatology produce a fatalistic, doom and gloom world view? Did it emphasize leaving the world rather than changing the world?

When Abraham paid tithes to Melchizedek he was acknowledging God's kingship rule over His life. His tithing unlocked God's Kingship economy (Genesis 14:19).

There can never be an "increase of His government" without the exercise of governing authority, dominion activity, and demonstrated kingship through His priest and kings (Isaiah 9:6-7).

We should never lead people to salvation and focus them solely on heaven (Revelation 5:10).

Chapter 12

KINGSHIP:
A FORWARD SHIFT

We can no longer sit idly by watching our world sink into moral decay and overcome by false religions. The Church is called to lead change and reform in our nation and throughout the earth. The Kingdom of God is not a future event. The Kingdom of God is here and now.

Kings are destined for total conquest. This world is desperate for good people like you to enter their kingship as an image bearer of Christ. Jesus loves this world and He has made provision for its restoration. You were born a winner. The whole world is waiting for you to exercise your believer's authority to act like a son of God (Romans 8:19).

Every member of the human race, whether he knows it or not, is a member of one of two kingdoms: the Kingdom of God or the kingdom of darkness. There is no middle or neutral ground. Scripture declares,

> "He that is not with me, is against me"
> (Matthew 12:12).

As kings we need to grab hold of our responsibility by invading this earth with God's purpose.

We have a kingship mandate; establish the Kingdom of God, right here and right now. An understanding of biblical influence and the kingship of every believer is a must. Kings apply God's Word to the land (Deuteronomy 16 & 17). Scripture uses the terms "salt" and "light" to teach us our responsibility to be proactive,

> "Ye are the salt of the earth: but if the salt has lost his savor, wherewith shall it be salted? It is thenceforth good for nothing, but to be cast out, and to be trodden under foot of men. Ye are the light of the world. A city that is set on a hill cannot be hid. Neither do men light a candle, and put it under a bushel, but on a

candlestick; and it giveth light unto all that are in the house. Let your light so shine before men, that they may see your good works, and glorify your Father which is in heaven" (Matthew 5:13-16).

We provide salt and light around us through kingship influence and by invading our society, and the world with the Gospel of the Kingdom.

Jesus taught us that the greatest in the Kingdom of God was a servant (Luke 22:26). We can become great servants by getting involved with Kingdom business. We can build schools, hospitals, clinics, banks, media outlets; we can become politically active, involved with international relief efforts, enter the business world, and a myriad of other such things. Tommy Reid in his book *Kingdom Now but Not Yet* said,

"The Bible must become more than a handbook of personal salvation. It must become a mandate for the reestablishment of Christ's rule and reign over the earth and the rebellious portion of the universe over which Satan now asserts dominion." [10]

PUSH TO THE FRONT

We can no longer sit idly by watching our world sink into moral decay and overcome by false religions. The Church is called to lead change and reform in our nation and throughout the earth (Ephesians 3:10). The Kingdom of God is not a future event but is now. John the Baptist proclaimed the coming Kingdom and Jesus announced its arrival (Matthew 3:2, 4:17; Mark 1:15).

Like John Calvin who went to Geneva to "establish the Kingdom of God in a decadent society," we too must involve ourselves with its establishment. Let's be like John the Baptist and make ready a people for God (Luke 1:16-17) and like Isaiah who prophesied of the anointing's purpose to "repair the waste cities that have been trodden down" (Isaiah 61:1-10).

You are in the Kingdom and the Kingdom is in you. When you exercise your authority as a king all other kingdoms must submit. The Kingdom of God can be seen by a demonstration of His Kingship in your life. Jesus said go and tell John the things you both hear and see (Luke 7:18-22). Jesus announced the reestablishment of His Kingship rule and government on earth and that was only the beginning, now you're involved.

Jesus came as the Second Adam to regain all His creation, many sons, and the earth. Now, through His priesthood of kings, He is restoring all things back to Himself. What a profound statement. Jesus had a revolutionary ministry. He preached the Kingdom of God, gave His life for the atonement of sin, birthed His Church, and planted a small seed that would grow and grow called the Kingdom of God. What's beautiful is that you and I, born again believers, can find our place and purpose in life. No longer are we wondering who we are or why we were born. We are a royal priesthood of kings being trained as representatives of His Kingdom government.

How exciting to know that we are being equipped to rule and reign with Christ on the earth, right here and right now. Throughout history God has been restoring truth to His Body, getting us ready to take dominion in His name. Just think about this, it took over 20 centuries to get us to a place where we could receive this truth about the kingship of Christ through His priesthood of kings. Jesus will return to the earth as the Lord (Ruler) Supreme for a glorious Church without spot nor wrinkle, not a defeated shadow lost in the umbers of defeat (Ephesians 5:27). You have been liberated and given talents to affect the world around you (Matthew

> Just think about this, it took over 20 centuries to get us to a place where we could receive this truth about the kingship of Christ through His priesthood of kings.

25:15). Determine in your heart to do something mighty with them.

CROSS AND KINGDOM

One day John the Baptist was in prison about to lose his life. He sent two disciples to Jesus asking Him,

> "Are you he that should come, or do we look for another? (Matthew 11:3).

Jesus answered saying,

> "Go and show John again those things which you do hear and see. The blind receive their sight, and the lame walk, the lepers are cleansed, and the deaf hear, the dead are raised up, and the poor have the Gospel preached to them. And blessed is he, whosoever shall not be offended in me" (Matthew 11:4-6).

I was wrongly taught that John asked that question because he was having a bad day. He was in prison filled with discouragement. But Jesus taught us something important about John's character. Jesus said that John was not like a reed that could be shaken in the wind. John wasn't staggering in unbelief. John knew who Jesus was. He knew that Jesus was the Messiah, the King of Glory. He knew that Jesus was Immanuel, God with us. John sent these two disciples to ask Jesus why He wasn't taking dominion. After all, the entire nation was waiting for the Messiah who would come and release the nation from the strongholds of Roman rule. Jesus preached about the Kingdom of God continually. Even the Pharisees came to Jesus demanding to know when the Kingdom of God would appear (Luke 17:20). In the days of Jesus' ministry everyone was looking at Christ's dominion and missed the cross of Calvary. Today, thousands of Gospel sermons are focused on the cross and miss the Kingdom. We need both.

TOTAL CONQUEST

Possessing God's promises requires a fighting spirit. Don't accept every thing that comes your way. Submit to God, engage all opposition to Christ's Kingship through you: invade, occupy and takeover. Then, after you have done all, stand rock solid in your faith refusing to break rank. Christ will not fail. You have been predestined for conquest.

We must stop acting like defeated second class citizens. This earth does not belong to Satan but to Jesus. We are destined for a victorious occupation. Jesus' prayer will be answered and we will see the establishment of the Kingdom of God on this earth (John 17:15-20). You are part of the army of the Lord and the army of the Lord is invincible. It's time to beat your plow shares into swords. You are not cursed, but blessed. Jesus didn't pray the Father to take His disciples out of the world but to protect them from the evil one. He said,

> "As thou hast sent me into the world, even so have I also sent them into the world" (John 17:18).

The apostolic reformation is restoring the truth of a kingship people with a kingship agenda. We are not being equipped to escape this world but to change it. Scripture teaches us the power of conquest in the parable of the leaven.

> "The kingdom of heaven is like unto leaven, which a woman took, and hid in three measures of meal, till the whole was leavened" (Matthew 13:33).

Notice the leaven didn't give up and quit, it was progressive in its work and destined to take over the entire meal. We, too, as a priesthood of kings, are destined for total conquest.

ACTION STEPS

What an exciting time to be alive. To make that forward shift into kingship start by acknowledging that Jesus has called you to be both salt and light in this world. Don't put your kingship under a bushel. You are a king because Jesus has made you a king. Now let your light shine. You have a bright future. As you step out in faith, know that you cannot fail. The Father is well pleased to give unto you the Kingdom. You are in the Kingdom and the Kingdom is in you. Arise, king, and give Jesus something to rejoice about.

CONCLUSION – IT'S A NEW DAY

Kingship is your path to a rich life full of success and significance. As life battles against you on your journey to Zion, remember what Sir Winston Churchill Prime Minister of the United Kingdom during the Second World War said, "Kites rise highest against the wind." You were born to win. You are a king and you were created for dominion.

> Kingship is your path to a rich life full of success and significance.

Push to the front of your calling and bring glory to your father. Jesus made it clear,

> "Verily, verily, I say unto you, he that believeth on me, the works that I do shall he do also and greater works than these shall he do because I go unto my Father" (John 14:12).

Let the kings arise!

APERÇU

Jesus loves this world and has made provision for its restoration.

Every member of the human race, whether he knows it or not, is a member of one of two kingdoms: the Kingdom of God or the kingdom of darkness. There is no middle or neutral ground. Scripture declares, "He that is not with me, is against me" (Matthew 12:12).

The Church is called to lead change and reform in our nation and throughout the earth (Ephesians 3:10).

The Kingdom of God can be seen by a demonstration of His Kingship in your life.

Jesus came as the Second Adam to regain all His creation, many sons and the earth. Now, through His priesthood of kings, He is restoring all things back to Himself.

We are a royal priesthood of kings being trained as enforcers of His Kingdom government.

The apostolic reformation is restoring the truth of a kingship people with a kingship mindset. We are not being equipped to escape this world but to change it.

Scripture teaches us the power of conquest in the parable of the leaven. "The kingdom of heaven is like unto leaven, which a woman took, and hid in three measures of meal, till the whole was leavened" (Matthew 13:33).

FOOTNOTES

Pg 50 - [1] Ladd, George Eldon. *The Gospel of the Kingdom.* The Paternoster Press, 1959

Pg 74 - [2] Dr. Bill Hamon, *The Day of the Saints*, P. 347, C 2002, Published by Destiny Image

Pg 92 - [3] Jessie Penn-Lewis, *War on the Saints,* Printed in England by Alfred Tacey Ltd. Excelsior Press, Leicester, 1912.

Pg 93 - [4] Colossians 2:15

Pg 111 - [5] Copeland, Kenneth, *John G. Lake His Life, His Sermons, His Boldness of Faith*, p.79, Published by Kenneth Copeland Publications, 1994

Pg 147 - [6] The Law of 72 is a mathematical formula that calculates the power of compound interest. Divide 72 by the prevailing interest rate to find how many years to double.

Pg 147 - [7] CardWeb.com

Pg 160 - [8] Monroe, Dr. Myles. Bahamas Faith Ministry. Destiny Image Publishers Inc. 2004

Pg 161 - [9] *What legacy is Left Behind? Is series' significance more than its profits?* by Melanie B. Smith, The Decatur Daily, Decatur, Alabama, 2005

Pg 177 - [10] *Kingdom Now But Not Yet*, Tommy Reid, 1988, IJN Publishing

APPENDIX

"KINGDOM OF GOD"
VERSE LIST – 70 SCRIPTURES

Matthew 6:33

"But seek ye first the kingdom of God and his righteousness, and all these things shall be added unto you."

Matthew 12:28

"But if I by the Spirit of God cast out demons, then indeed the kingdom of God is come upon you."

Matthew 19:24

"And again I say unto you, It is easier for a camel to enter a needle's eye than a rich man into the kingdom of God."

Matthew 21:31

"Which of the two did the will of the father? They said to him, the first. Jesus said to them, Verily I say unto you that the tax-gatherers and the harlots go into the kingdom of God before you."

Matthew 21:43

"Therefore I say to you, that the kingdom of God shall be taken from you and shall be given to a nation producing the fruits of it."

Mark 1:14

"But after John was delivered up, Jesus came into Galilee preaching the glad tidings of the kingdom of God..."

Mark 1:15

"And saying, the time is fulfilled and the kingdom of God has drawn nigh; repent and believe in the glad tidings."

Mark 4:11

"And he said to them, To you is given to know the mystery of the kingdom of God; but to them who are without, all things are done in parables..."

Mark 4:26

"And he said, thus is the kingdom of God, as if a man should cast the seed upon the earth..."

Mark 4:30

"And he said, how should we liken the kingdom of God, or with what comparison should we compare it?"

Mark 9:1

"And he said to them, Verily I say unto you, there are some of those standing here that shall not taste death until they shall have seen the kingdom of God come in power."

Mark 9:47

"And if thine eye serve as a snare to thee, cast it out: it is better for thee to enter into the kingdom of God with one eye, rather than having two eyes to be cast into the hell of fire…"

Mark 10:14

"But Jesus seeing it, was indignant, and said to them, suffer the little children to come to me; forbid them not; for of such is the kingdom of God."

Mark 10:15

"Verily I say to you, whosoever shall not receive the kingdom of God as a little child, shall in no wise enter into it."

Mark 10:23

"And Jesus looking around said to his disciples, how difficult shall they that have riches enter into the kingdom of God!"

Mark 10:24

"And the disciples were amazed at his words. And Jesus again answering said to them, Children, how difficult it is that those who trust in riches should enter into the kingdom of God!"

Mark 10:25

"It is easier for a camel to go through the eye of a needle than for a rich man to enter into the kingdom of God."

Mark 12:34

"And Jesus, seeing that he had answered intelligently, said to him, Thou art not far from the kingdom of God. And no one dared question him any more."

Mark 14:25

"Verily I say to you, I will no more drink at all of the fruit of the vine, until that day when I drink it new in the kingdom of God."

Mark 15:43

"Joseph of Arimathaea, an honorable councilor, who also himself was awaiting the kingdom of God, coming, emboldened himself and went in to Pilate and begged the body of Jesus."

Luke 4:43

"But he said to them, I must needs announce the glad tidings of the kingdom of God to the other cities also, for this I have been sent forth."

Luke 6:20

"And he, lifting up his eyes upon his disciples, said, blessed are ye poor, for yours is the kingdom of God."

Luke 7:28

"For I say unto you, Among them that are born of women a greater prophet is no one than John the baptist; but he who is a little one in the kingdom of God is greater than he."

Luke 8:1

"And it came to pass afterwards that he went through the country city by city, and village by village, preaching and announcing the glad tidings of the kingdom of God; and the twelve were with him…"

Luke 8:10

"And he said, to you it is given to know the mysteries of the kingdom of God, but to the rest in parables, in order that seeing they may not see, and hearing they may not understand."

Luke 9:2

"And sent them to proclaim the kingdom of God and to heal the sick."

Luke 9:11

"But the crowds knowing it followed him; and he received them and spake to them of the kingdom of God, and cured those that had need of healing."

Luke 9:27

"But I say unto you of a truth, there are some of those standing here who shall not taste death until they shall have seen the kingdom of God."

Luke 9:60

"But Jesus said to him, suffer the dead to bury their own dead, but do thou go and announce the kingdom of God."

Luke 9:62

"But Jesus said to him, no one having laid his hand on the plough and looking back is fit for the kingdom of God."

Luke 10:9

"And heal the sick in it, and say to them, the kingdom of God is come nigh to you."

Luke 10:11

"Even the dust of your city, which cleaves to us on the feet, do we shake off against you; but know this, that the kingdom of God is come nigh."

Luke 11:20

"But if by the finger of God I cast out demons, then the kingdom of God is come upon you."

Luke 12:31

"But seek his kingdom, and all these things shall be added to you."

Luke 13:18

"And he said, to what is the kingdom of God like? And to what shall I liken it?"

Luke 13:20

"And again he said, to what shall I liken the kingdom of God?"

Luke 13:28

"There shall be the weeping and the gnashing of teeth, when ye shall see Abraham and Isaac and Jacob and all the prophets in the kingdom of God, but yourselves cast out."

Luke 13:29

"And they shall come from east and west, and from north and south, and shall lie down at table in the kingdom of God."

Luke 14:15

"And one of those that were lying at table with them, hearing these things, said to him, blessed is he who shall eat bread in the kingdom of God."

Luke 16:16

"The law and the prophets were until John: from that time the glad tidings of the kingdom of God are announced, and every one forces his way into it."

Luke 17:20

"And having been asked by the Pharisees, When is the kingdom of God coming? He answered them and said, the kingdom of God does not come with observation..."

Luke 17:21

"Nor shall they say, Lo here, or, Lo there; for behold, the kingdom of God is in the midst of you."

Luke 18:16

"But Jesus calling them to him said, Suffer little children to come to me, and do not forbid them, for of such is the kingdom of God."

Luke 18:17

"Verily I say to you, whosoever shall not receive the kingdom of God as a little child shall in no wise enter therein."

Luke 18:24

"But when Jesus saw that he became very sorrowful, he said, how hardly shall those who have riches enter into the kingdom of God!"

Luke 18:25

"For it is easier for a camel to enter through a needle's eye than for a rich man to enter into the kingdom of God."

Luke 18:29

"And he said to them, Verily I say to you, There is no one who has left home, or parents, or brethren, or wife, or children, for the kingdom of God's sake..."

Luke 19:11

"But as they were listening to these things, he added and spake a parable, because he was near to Jerusalem and they thought that the kingdom of God was about to be immediately manifested."

Luke 21:31

"So also ye, when ye see these things take place, know that the kingdom of God is near."

Luke 22:16

"For I say unto you, that I will not eat any more at all of it until it be fulfilled in the kingdom of God."

Luke 22:18

"For I say unto you, that I will not drink at all of the fruit of the vine until the kingdom of God come."

Luke 23:51

"(This man had not assented to their counsel and deed), of Arimathaea, a city of the Jews, who also waited, himself also, for the kingdom of God."

John 3:3

"Jesus answered and said to him, Verily, verily, I say unto thee, except any one be born anew he cannot see the kingdom of God."

John 3:5

"Jesus answered, Verily, verily, I say unto thee, except any one be born of water and of Spirit, he cannot enter into the kingdom of God."

Acts 1:3

"To whom also he presented himself living, after he had suffered, with many proofs; being seen by them during forty days, and speaking of the things which concern the kingdom of God..."

Acts 8:12

"But when they believed Philip announcing the glad tidings concerning the kingdom of God and the name of Jesus Christ, they were baptized, both men and women."

Acts 14:22

"Establishing the souls of the disciples, exhorting them to abide in the faith, and that through many tribulations we must enter into the kingdom of God."

Acts 19:8

"And entering into the synagogue, he spoke boldly during three months, reasoning and persuading the things concerning the kingdom of God."

Acts 20:25

"And now, behold, I know that ye all, among whom I have gone about preaching the kingdom of God, shall see my face no more."

Acts 28:23

"And having appointed him a day many came to him to the lodging, to whom he expounded, testifying of the kingdom of God, and persuading them concerning Jesus, both from the law of Moses and the prophets, from early morning to evening."

Acts 28:31

"Preaching the kingdom of God, and teaching the things concerning the Lord Jesus Christ, with all freedom unhindered."

Romans 14:17

"For the kingdom of God is not eating and drinking, but righteousness, and peace, and joy in the Holy Spirit."

1 Corinthians 4:20

"For the kingdom of God is not in word, but in power."

1 Corinthians 6:9

"Do ye not know that unrighteous persons shall not inherit the kingdom of God? Do not err: neither fornicators, nor idolaters, nor adulterers, nor those who make women of themselves, nor who abuse themselves with men…"

1 Corinthians 6:10

"Nor thieves, nor covetous, nor drunkards, nor abusive persons, nor the rapacious, shall inherit the kingdom of God."

1 Corinthians 15:50

"But this I say, brethren, that flesh and blood cannot inherit God's kingdom, nor does corruption inherit incorruptibility."

Galatians 5:21

"Envyings, murders, drunkennesses, revels, and things like these; as to which I tell you beforehand, even as I also have said before, that they who do such things shall not inherit God's kingdom."

Colossians 4:11

"And Jesus called Justus, who are of the circumcision. These are the only fellow-workers for the kingdom of God who have been a consolation to me."

2 Thessalonians 1:5

"A manifest token of the righteous judgment of God, to the end that ye should be counted worthy of the kingdom of God, for the sake of which ye also suffer…"

"KINGDOM OF HEAVEN" VERSE LIST – 33 SCRIPTURES

Matthew 3:2

"And saying, Repent, for the kingdom of heaven has drawn nigh."

Matthew 4:17

"From that time began Jesus to preach and to say, Repent, for the kingdom of heaven has drawn nigh."

Matthew 5:3

"Blessed are the poor in spirit, for theirs is the kingdom of heaven."

Matthew 5:10

"Blessed they who are persecuted on account of righteousness, for theirs is the kingdom of heaven."

Matthew 5:19

"Whosoever then shall do away with one of these least commandments, and shall teach men so, shall be called least in the kingdom of the heaven; but whosoever shall practice and teach them, he shall be called great in the kingdom of heaven."

Matthew 5:20

"For I say unto you, that unless your righteousness surpasses that of the scribes and Pharisees, ye shall in no wise enter into the kingdom of heaven."

Matthew 7:21

"Not every one who says to me, Lord, Lord, shall enter into the kingdom of the heaven, but he that does the will of my Father who is in heaven."

Matthew 8:11

"But I say unto you, that many shall come from the rising and setting sun, and shall lie down at table with Abraham, and Isaac, and Jacob in the kingdom of heaven…"

Matthew 10:7

"And as ye go, preach, saying, the kingdom of heaven has drawn nigh."

Matthew 11:11

"Verily I say to you, that there is not arisen among the born of women a greater than John the Baptist. But he who is a little one in the kingdom of heaven is greater than he."

Matthew 11:12

"But from the days of John the Baptist until now, the kingdom of the heaven is taken by violence, and the violent seize on it."

Matthew 13:11

"And he answering said to them, because to you it is given to know the mysteries of the kingdom of heaven, but to them it is not given…"

Matthew 13:24

"Another parable set he before them, saying, The kingdom of heaven has become like a man sowing good seed in his field…"

Matthew 13:31

"Another parable set he before them, saying, The kingdom of heaven is like a grain of mustard seed which a man took and sowed in his field…"

Matthew 13:33

"He spoke another parable to them: The kingdom of heaven is like leaven, which a woman took and hid in three measures of meal until it had been all leavened."

Matthew 13:44

"The kingdom of heaven is like a treasure hid in the field, which a man having found has hid, and for the joy of it goes and sells all whatever he has, and buys that field."

Matthew 13:45

"Again, the kingdom of heaven is like a merchant seeking beautiful pearls…"

Matthew 13:47

"Again, the kingdom of heaven is like a seine which has been cast into the sea, and which has gathered together of every kind…"

Matthew 13:52

"And he said to them, for this reason every scribe discipled to the kingdom of heaven is like a man that is a householder who brings out of his treasure things new and old."

Matthew 16:19

"And I will give to thee the keys of the Kingdom of the heaven; and whatsoever thou mayest bind upon the earth shall be bound in heaven; and whatsoever thou mayest loose on the earth shall be loosed in heaven."

Matthew 18:1

"In that hour the disciples came to Jesus saying, who then is greatest in the kingdom of heaven?"

Matthew 18:3

"And said, Verily I say to you, unless ye are converted and become as little children, ye will not at all enter into the kingdom of heaven."

Matthew 18:4

"Whoever therefore shall humble himself as this little child, he is the greatest in the kingdom of heaven…"

Matthew 18:23

"For this cause the kingdom of heaven has become like a king who would reckon with his bondmen."

Matthew 19:12

"For there are eunuchs which have been born thus from their mother's womb; and there are eunuchs who have been made eunuchs of men; and there are eunuchs who have made eunuchs of themselves for the sake of the kingdom of heaven. He that is able to receive it, let him receive it."

Matthew 19:14

"But Jesus said, Suffer little children, and do not hinder them from coming to me; for the kingdom of heaven is of such:"

Matthew 19:23

"And Jesus said to his disciples, Verily I say unto you, A rich man shall with difficulty enter into the kingdom of heaven…"

Matthew 20:1

"For the kingdom of heaven is like a householder who went out with the early morn to hire workmen for his vineyard."

Matthew 22:2

"The kingdom of heaven has become like a king who made a wedding feast for his son…"

Matthew 23:13

"But woe unto you, scribes and Pharisees, hypocrites, for ye shut up the kingdom of heaven before men; for ye do not enter, nor do ye suffer those that are entering to go in."

Matthew 25:1

"Then shall the kingdom of heaven be made like to ten virgins that having taken their torches, went forth to meet the bridegroom."

Matthew 25:14

"For the kingdom of heaven is as a man going away out of a country who called his own servants and delivered unto them his goods."

THE SEVEN PARABLES
OF THE KINGDOM

1. The Word Of The Kingdom Is Sown In
   Three Different Types of Soils
   Matthew 13:3-23

2. In The Kingdom Of God Wheat And
   Tares Grow Together Until...
   Matthew 13:24-30

3. The Kingdom Of God Is Like A Grain
   Of Mustard Seed – Starts Small And Ends Big
   Matthew 13:34-43

4. The Kingdom Is Like Leaven – Total Conquest
   Matthew 13:33-35

5. The Kingdom Of God Is Like A Treasure
   Hidden In A Field
   Matthew 13:44

6. The Kingdom Of God Is Like A Pearl Of
   Great Value – Priceless
   Matthew 13:45-46

7. The Kingdom Of God Is Like A Net
   Gathering All Kinds – For All
   Matthew 13:47-52

INVITATION TO DESTINY

Are you hungry for more of God? In addition to preaching the Gospel around the world, we also pastor a powerful, Spirit-filled church in South Florida. The Spirit of God told us to build a church from which to send forth believers that could reach their cities and impact the nations for Jesus Christ.

Have you been searching for God only to find religion? Spirit of Life Ministries (SOLM) is a multi-cultural church where all races gather together in unity and cares for the needs of the whole family. Is something missing from your life? SOLM is a church where you can receive what you need from the Lord. We believe in divine healing, manifesting the gifts of the Spirit, prayer results, miracles, prosperity, finding purpose and making a difference. With God all things are possible.

Are you looking for a place to grow? SOLM is a new apostolic church with all five-fold ministry gifts operating. We have a prophetic call and mandate to equip, activate and release every believer into the work of the ministry according to Ephesians 4:11-12. We invite you to come and connect with your destiny and receive confirmation, impartation and activation for your life.

Come adventure with us,

Jonas and Rhonda Clark

SPIRIT OF LIFE MINISTRIES WORLD HEADQUARTERS
27 WEST HALLANDALE BEACH BLVD. • HALLANDALE BEACH, FLA. 33009
800.943.6490 • WWW.JONASCLARK.COM

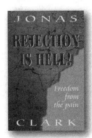

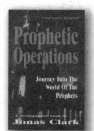
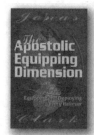
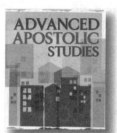

Want to know more about the Kingdom of God?

Find answers in THE VOICE® magazine.

Sign up to receive a
FREE Issue of THE VOICE® magazine
at www.thevoicemagazine.com

JONAS CLARK'S REVOLUTIONARY REVIEW

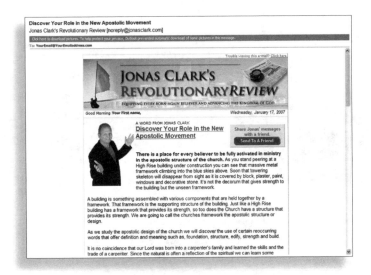

Receive bi-weekly FREE articles
from Jonas Clark to equip you for your destiny.
Read present truth articles on topics such
as apostolic ministry, spritual warfare,
deliverance, prophetic ministry, Kingdom
living and more.

Sign up today @
www.JonasClark.com